Steck-Vaughn

English ASAP™

Connecting English to the Workplace

SCANS Consultant

Shirley Brod
Workforce ESL Consultant
Boulder, Colorado

Program Consultants

Judith Dean-Griffin
ESL Teacher
Windham Independent School District
Texas Department of Criminal Justice
Huntsville, Texas

Marilyn K. Spence
Workforce Education Coordinator
Orange Technical Education Centers
Mid-Florida Tech
Orlando, Florida

Brigitte Marshall
English Language Training
for Employment Participation
Albany, California

Christine Kay Williams
ESL Specialist
Towson University
Baltimore, Maryland

Marcia L. Taylor
ESL Basic Skills Instructor
JobLink 2000
Employee Learning Center
ISPAT Inland Steel Company
East Chicago, Indiana

STECK-VAUGHN®
C O M P A N Y

A Division of Harcourt Brace & Company

www.steck-vaughn.com

Acknowledgments

Executive Editor:	Ellen Northcutt
Supervising Editor:	Tim Collins
Assistant Art Director:	Richard Balsam
Interior Design:	Richard Balsam, Jill Klinger, Paul Durick
Electronic Production:	Rebecca Gonzales, Katie Keenan
Assets Manager:	Margie Foster

Photo Credits

Randal Alhadeff–p.3c, 15b, 15c, 16d, 27c, 34-35, 39a, 39b, 41, 46-47, 51b, 56, 58-59, 63a, 63d, 80, 83a, 83b, 83c, 83d, 83e, 83f, 87c, 87d, 94-95, 99c, 106-107, 111d, 113, 118-119; Don Couch–p.5, 16a, 28b, 28c, 51a, 75a, 90a, 90b; Christine Galida–p.15d, 27a, 87b; Ken Lax–p.51c, 54, 75b, 99d; David Omer–p.22-23, 82-83; Park Street–p.3a, 3d, 10-11, 15a, 27b, 39c, 70-71, 75d, 89, 99a, 99b, 111c; Ken Walker–p.3b, 16b, 16c, 28a, 50, 51d, 63b, 63c; Rick Williams–p.22, 24, 27d, 39d, 75c, 87a, 101, 102, 111a.

Additional photography: P. 111b ©Mark Richards/PhotoEdit.

Illustration Credits

Cover: Tim Dove, D Childress

Cindy Aarvig, Richard Balsam, Barbara Beck/Integrity Graphics, David Griffin, Layne Johnson, Chuck Joseph, Linda Kelen, Michael Krone, Gordon Ricke, Joel Snyder/Publishers' Graphics, Danielle Szabo/kreativ design, Victoria Vebell.

Contents

Unit	SCANS Competencies	Workforce Skills
Unit 1 **Communication**	Acquire and evaluate information Interpret and communicate information Organize information Improve systems	Summarize information Put information in order Ask for information Interpret information
Unit 2 **Your Workplace**	Interpret and communicate information Understand organizational systems Monitor and correct performance Work on teams	Describe your job duties Explain why your job is important Transfer your skills to a better job Learn from experience
Unit 3 **Technology**	Apply technology to specific tasks Acquire and evaluate information Select equipment and tools Understand technological systems Use computers to process information	Put information in a computer Get information from a computer Understand information from a computer Use information from a computer
Unit 4 **Time** **Management**	Allocate time Select equipment and tools Work on teams Understand organizational systems Monitor and correct performance	Set long-term and short-term goals Deal with setbacks Set priorities Avoid procrastination
Unit 5 **Customer** **Service**	Serve customers Interpret and communicate information Solve problems Improve systems	Respond positively to customers' complaints Solve customers' problems Evaluate advice about customer service Improve customer service
Unit 6 **Culture of Work**	Understand organizational systems Communicate information Work on teams Allocate staff Design and improve systems	Understand how your workplace is organized Identify bosses, coworkers, and direct reports Identify training needs Develop a plan for solving a problem
Unit 7 **Finances**	Interpret information Allocate money Evaluate data	Interpret and evaluate a budget Create a budget Adjust a budget Make decisions on a budget
Unit 8 **Health and** **Safety**	Monitor and correct performance Select equipment and tools Interpret information	Identify health and safety problems Solve health and safety problems Improve health and safety
Unit 9 **Working with** **People**	Acquire and evaluate data Monitor and correct performance Design or improve systems Lead	Confirm information before you act Demonstrate leadership skills Adjust to change
Unit 10 **Career** **Development**	Acquire and evaluate data Allocate time Understand organizational systems Monitor performance	Evaluate job performance Assess your work skills Plan for the future

Each unit of *English ASAP* systematically presents one or more SCANS Competencies.
The SCANS Foundation Skills are integrated throughout the instruction.

Unit	Grammar
Unit 1 **Communication**	Review of past tenses (simple past, past progressive) Clauses with **when** and **while** **Used to** (statements, questions)
Unit 2 **Your Workplace**	Review of present tenses (present tense of **be**, simple present, present progressive) **Feel** (review)
Unit 3 **Technology**	Simple past tense with **ago** (review) Present perfect tense with **for** and since Questions with **how long**
Unit 4 **Time Management**	Passive voice (simple present, simple past) Gerunds as objects
Unit 5 **Customer Service**	Gerunds after **by** and **without** **By, with,** and **without** + noun
Unit 6 **Culture of Work**	**Wh-** questions (review) Restrictive relative clauses
Unit 7 **Finances**	**Must/may** Gerunds as subjects Conditional sentences with **could**
Unit 8 **Health and Safety**	**Must be** (possibility) **Should, ought to, had better** (advice)
Unit 9 **Working with People**	Gerunds as subjects and objects (review) Present and past participles
Unit 10 **Career Development**	Review of tenses

Introduction to English ASAP

English ASAP is a complete, communicative, SCANS-based, four-skill ESL program for teaching adult and young adult learners the skills they need to succeed at work.

FEATURES

♦ *English ASAP* **is SCANS-based.** *English ASAP*'s SCANS-based syllabus teaches skills learners need to succeed in the workplace. The syllabus is correlated with the SCANS competencies, a taxonomy of work skills recognized by the U.S. Department of Labor as essential to every job. Additionally, the syllabus is compatible with the work skills and competencies in the Comprehensive Adult Student Assessment System (CASAS) Competencies, the Mainstream English Language Training Project (MELT), the National Institute for Literacy's Equipped for the Future Framework for Adult Literacy, and state curriculums for adult ESL from Texas and California.

 The *On Your Job* symbol appears on the Student Book page and corresponding page in the Teacher's Edition each time learners apply a SCANS-based skill to their jobs or career interests.

♦ *English ASAP* **is about the world of work.** All of the conversations, reading selections, listening activities, and realia are drawn from authentic workplace situations. *English ASAP* presents settings and workers from major career clusters, including transportation, health care, service occupations, office occupations, construction, hospitality, and industrial occupations.

♦ *English ASAP* **teaches the skills required in all job descriptions.** Learners gain valuable experience working in teams; teaching others; serving customers; organizing, evaluating, and communicating information; understanding and using technology; negotiating; allocating resources; and completing projects.

♦ *English ASAP* **is communicative.** Numerous conversational models and communicative activities in the Student Books and Teacher's Editions—including problem-solving activities, surveys, and cooperative learning projects—get learners talking from the start.

♦ **English ASAP is appropriate for adults and young adults.** The language and situations presented in *English ASAP* are ones adults and young adults are likely to encounter. The abundance of attractive, true-to-life photographs, illustrations, and realia will interest and motivate adult and young adult learners.

♦ *English ASAP* **addresses all four language skills.** Each level of *English ASAP* addresses listening, speaking, reading, and writing. Starting in Level 1, a two-page grammar spread in each Student Book unit plus corresponding Workbook reinforcement and supplementary grammar worksheets in the Teacher's Editions ensure that learners get appropriate grammar practice.

♦ *English ASAP* **starts at the true beginner level.** *English ASAP* begins at the Literacy Level, designed for learners who have no prior knowledge of English and have few or no literacy skills in their native language(s) or are literate in a language with a non-Roman alphabet. Learners master foundation literacy skills in tandem with listening and speaking skills. The next level, Level 1, is intended for learners with little or no prior knowledge of English. As learners continue through the program, they master progressively higher levels of language and work skills. The Placement Tests help teachers place learners in the appropriate level of the program. For information on placement, see page v of this Teacher's Edition.

♦ *English ASAP* **is appropriate for multilevel classes.** Because unit topics carry over from level to level with increasing sophistication, the series is ideal for use in multilevel classes. For example, a Literacy Level skill in the technology unit is naming machines. A Level 2 skill in the technology unit is completing machine maintenance reports. Units are situational and nonsequential, making *English ASAP* appropriate for open-entry/open-exit situations.

♦ *English ASAP* **meets the needs of individual workplaces and learners.** Because the demands of each workplace and each individual's job are unique, the abundance of *On Your Job* activities allows learners to relate their new skills to their workplaces and career interests. In addition, the Personal Dictionary feature in each unit lets learners focus only on the vocabulary they need to do their jobs. Finally, with Steck-Vaughn's *Workforce Writing Dictionary,* learners can create a complete custom dictionary of all the vocabulary they need to know to succeed.

COMPONENTS

English ASAP consists of:

♦ Student Books

♦ Workbooks starting at Level 1

♦ Teacher's Editions

♦ Audiocassettes

♦ Steck-Vaughn *Workforce Writing Dictionary*

♦ Placement Tests, Form A and Form B

Student Books

Each four-color Student Book consists of ten 12-page units, providing learners with ample time on task to acquire the target SCANS competencies and language.

♦ **The Student Books follow a consistent format for easy teaching and learning.** Each unit is consistently organized and can be taught in approximately eight to twelve classroom sessions.

♦ **Complete front matter offers valuable teaching suggestions.** Ideas on how to teach each type of activity in the Student Book units and suggested teaching techniques give teachers valuable information on how to use *English ASAP* with maximum success.

♦ **Clear directions and abundant examples ensure that learners always know exactly what to do.** Examples for each activity make tasks apparent to learners and teachers. Clear exercise titles and directions tell teachers and learners exactly what learners are to do.

♦ **Performance Check pages provide a complete evaluation program.** Teachers can use these pages to evaluate learners' progress and to track the program's learner verification needs. Success is built in because work skills are always checked in familiar formats.

Workbooks

The Workbooks contain ten eight-page units plus a complete Answer Key. Each Workbook unit always contains at least one exercise for each section of the Student Book. To allow for additional reinforcement of grammar, there are multiple exercises for the Grammar section. The exercises for each section of the Student Book are indicated on the corresponding page of the Teacher's Edition and in a chart at the front of each Workbook. Because the Answer Keys are removable, the Workbooks can be used both in the classroom and for self-study.

Teacher's Editions

The complete Teacher's Editions help both new and experienced teachers organize their teaching, motivate their learners, and successfully use a variety of individual, partner, and teamwork activities.

♦ **Unit Overviews provide valuable information on how to motivate learners and organize teaching.** Each opener contains a complete list of the SCANS and workplace skills in the unit to help teachers organize their teaching. The Unit Warm-Up on each unit opener page helps teachers build learners' interest and gets them ready for the unit. The openers also contain a list of materials—including pictures, flash cards, and realia—teachers can use to enliven instruction throughout the unit.

♦ **The Teacher's Editions contain complete suggested preparation and teaching procedures for each section of the Student Book.** Each section of a unit begins with a list of the workplace skills developed on the Student Book page(s). Teachers can use the list when planning lessons. The teaching notes give suggestions for a recommended three-part lesson format:

Preparation: Suggestions for preteaching the new language, SCANS skills, and concepts on the Student Book page(s) before learners open their books.

Presentation: Suggested procedures for working with the Student Book page(s) in class.

Follow-Up: An optional activity to provide reinforcement or to enrich and extend the new language and competencies. The Follow-Ups include a variety of interactive partner and team activities. Each activity has a suggested variant, marked with ♦, for use with learners who require activities at a slightly more sophisticated level. For teaching ease, the corresponding Workbook exercise(s) for each page or section of the Student Book are indicated on the Teacher's Edition page starting at Level 1.

♦ **The Teacher's Editions contain SCANS Notes, Teaching Notes, Culture Notes, and Language Notes.** Teachers can share this wealth of information with learners or use it in lesson planning.

♦ **Each Teacher's Edition unit contains an additional suggested Informal Workplace-Specific Assessment.** Teachers will find these suggestions invaluable in evaluating learners' success in relating their new skills to their workplaces or career interests. Designed to supplement the Performance Check pages in each unit of the Student

Books, these brief speaking activities include having learners state their workplace's customer service policies, their workplace's policies on lateness and absence, and the procedures they use at work to maintain equipment.

♦ **Blackline Masters.** In the Literacy Level, the Blackline Masters help teachers present or reinforce many basic literacy skills. Starting at Level 1, the Blackline Masters reinforce the grammar in each unit.

♦ **Additional features in the Teacher's Editions.** The Teacher's Editions contain Individual Competency Charts for each unit and a Class Cumulative Competency Chart for recording learners' progress and tracking the program's learner verification needs. A Certificate of Completion is included for teachers to copy and award to learners upon successful completion of that level of *English ASAP*. In addition, each unit of the Literacy Level Teacher's Edition contains an ASAP Project, an optional holistic cooperative learning project. Learners will find these to be valuable and stimulating culminating activities. Starting at Level 1, the ASAP Project appears directly on the Student Book pages.

Audiocassettes

The audiocassettes contain all the dialogs and listening activities marked with this cassette symbol. The audiocassettes provide experience in listening to a variety of native speakers in the workplace. The Listening Transcript at the back of each Student Book and Teacher's Edition contains the scripts of all the listening selections not appearing directly on the pages of the Student Books.

Workforce Writing Dictionary

The Steck-Vaughn *Workforce Writing Dictionary* is a 96-page custom dictionary that lets learners create a personalized, alphabetical list of words and expressions related to their own workplaces and career interests. Each letter of the alphabet is allocated two to four pages and is illustrated with several workforce-related words. Learners can use the dictionary to record all of the relevant language they need to succeed on their jobs.

Placement Tests

The Placement Tests, Form A and Form B, help teachers place learners in the appropriate level of *English ASAP*. For more information see page v of this Teacher's Edition.

About SCANS

Each unit of *English ASAP* systematically presents one or more SCANS Competencies. The Foundation Skills are integrated through all the instruction.

WORKPLACE KNOW-HOW

The know-how identified by SCANS is made up of five competencies and a three-part foundation of skills and personal qualities needed for solid job performance. These include:

COMPETENCIES—effective workers can productively use:

- **Resources**—allocating time, money, materials, space, staff;

- **Interpersonal Skills**—working on teams, teaching others, serving customers, leading, negotiating, and working well with people from culturally diverse backgrounds;

- **Information**—acquiring and evaluating data, organizing and maintaining files, interpreting and communicating, and using computers to process information;

- **Systems**—understanding social, organizational, and technological systems, monitoring and correcting performance, and designing or improving systems;

- **Technology**—selecting equipment and tools, applying technology to specific tasks, and maintaining and troubleshooting technologies.

THE FOUNDATION—competence requires:

- **Basic Skills**—reading, writing, arithmetic and mathematics, speaking and listening;

- **Thinking Skills**—thinking creatively, making decisions, solving problems, seeing things in the mind's eye, knowing how to learn, and reasoning;

- **Personal Qualities**—individual responsibility, self-esteem, sociability, self-management, and integrity.

Reprinted from *What Work Requires of Schools—A SCANS Report for America 2000,* Secretary's Commission on Achieving Necessary Skills, U.S. Department of Labor.

For Additional Information

For more information on SCANS, CASAS, adult literacy, and the workforce, visit these websites.

CASAS Information

www.casas.org

Center for Applied Linguistics

www.cal.org

Education Information

www.ed.gov

Literacy Link

www.pbs.org/learn/literacy

National Center on Adult Literacy

www.literacyonline.org/ncal/index.html

National Institute for Literacy

novel.nifl.gov

School-to-Work Information

www.stw.ed.gov

Workforce Information

www.doleta.gov

Workforce Investment Act

www.usworkforce.org

www.icesa.org

For more information about Steck-Vaughn, visit our website.

www.steckvaughn.com

Steck-Vaughn

English ASAP™

Connecting English to the Workplace

SCANS Consultant

Shirley Brod
Workforce ESL Consultant
Boulder, Colorado

Program Consultants

Judith Dean-Griffin
ESL Teacher
Windham Independent School District
Texas Department of Criminal Justice
Huntsville, Texas

Marilyn K. Spence
Workforce Education Coordinator
Orange Technical Education Centers
Mid-Florida Tech
Orlando, Florida

Brigitte Marshall
English Language Training
for Employment Participation
Albany, California

Christine Kay Williams
ESL Specialist
Towson University
Baltimore, Maryland

Marcia L. Taylor
ESL Basic Skills Instructor
JobLink 2000
Employee Learning Center
ISPAT Inland Steel Company
East Chicago, Indiana

STECK-VAUGHN
C O M P A N Y

A Division of Harcourt Brace & Company

www.steck-vaughn.com

About SCANS, the Workforce, and *English ASAP: Connecting English to the Workplace*

SCANS and the Workforce

The Secretary's Commission on Achieving Necessary Skills (SCANS) was established by the U.S. Department of Labor in 1990. Its mission was to study the demands of workplace environments and determine whether people entering the workforce are capable of meeting those demands. The commission identified skills for employment, suggested ways for assessing proficiency, and devised strategies to implement the identified skills. The commission's first report, entitled *What Work Requires of Schools—SCANS Report for America 2000*, was published in June 1991. The report is designed for use by educators (curriculum developers, job counselors, training directors, and teachers) to prepare the modern workforce for the workplace with viable, up-to-date skills.

The report identified two types of skills: Competencies and Foundations. There are five SCANS Competencies: (1) Resources, (2) Interpersonal, (3) Information, (4) Systems, and (5) Technology. There are three parts contained in SCANS Foundations: (1) Basic Skills (including reading, writing, arithmetic, mathematics, listening, and speaking); (2) Thinking Skills (including creative thinking, decision making, problem solving, seeing things in the mind's eye, knowing how to learn, and reasoning); and (3) Personal Qualities (including responsibility, self-esteem, sociability, self-management, and integrity/honesty).

Steck-Vaughn's *English ASAP: Connecting English to the Workplace*

English ASAP is a complete SCANS-based, four-skills program for teaching ESL and SCANS skills to adults and young adults. *English ASAP* follows a work skills-based syllabus that is compatible with the CASAS and MELT competencies.

English ASAP is designed for learners enrolled in public or private schools, in corporate training environments, in learning centers, or in institutes, and for individuals working with tutors. *English ASAP* has these components:

Student Books

The Student Books are designed to allow from 125 to 235 hours of instruction. Each Student Book contains 10 units of SCANS-based instruction. A Listening Transcript of material appearing on the Audiocassettes and a Vocabulary list, organized by unit, of core workforce-based words and phrases appear at the back of each Student Book. Because unit topics carry over from level to level, *English ASAP* is ideal for multi-level classes.

The *On Your Job* symbol appears on the Student Book page each time learners apply a work skill to their own jobs or career interests.

An abundance of tips throughout each unit provides information and strategies that learners can use to be more effective workers and language learners.

Teacher's Editions

Teacher's Editions provide reduced Student Book pages with answers inserted and wraparound teacher notes that give detailed suggestions on how to present each page of the Student Book in class. Starting at Level 1, the Teacher's Editions also provide blackline masters to reinforce the grammar in each unit. The Literacy Level Teacher's Edition contains blackline masters that provide practice with many basic literacy skills. The complete Listening Transcript, Vocabulary, and charts for tracking individual and class success appear at the back of each Teacher's Edition.

Workbooks

The Workbooks, starting at Level 1, provide reinforcement for each section of the Student Books.

Audiocassettes

The Audiocassettes contain all the dialogs and listening activities in the Student Books.

 This symbol appears on the Student Book page and corresponding Teacher's Edition page each time material for that page is recorded on the Audiocassettes. A Listening Transcript of all material recorded on the tapes but not appearing directly on the Student Book pages is at the back of each Student Book and Teacher's Edition.

Workforce Writing Dictionary

Steck-Vaughn's *Workforce Writing Dictionary*, is a 96-page custom dictionary that allows learners to create a personalized, alphabetical list of the key words and phrases they need to know for their jobs. Each letter of the alphabet is allocated two to four pages for learners to record the language they need. In addition, each letter is illustrated with several workforce-related words.

Placement Tests

The Placement Tests, Form A and Form B, can be used as entry and exit tests and to assist in placing learners in the appropriate level of *English ASAP*.

Placement

In addition to the Placement Tests, the following table indicates placement based on the CASAS and new MELT student performance level standards.

Placement

New MELT SPL	CASAS Achievement Score	English ASAP
0–1	179 or under	Literacy
2–3	180–200	Level 1
4–5	201–220	Level 2
6	221–235	Level 3
7	236 and above	Level 4

About Student Book 4

Organization of a Unit

Each twelve-page unit contains these nine sections: Unit Opener, Getting Started, Talk About It, Keep Talking, Listening, Grammar, Reading and Writing, Extension, and Performance Check.

Unit Opener

Each Unit Opener includes photos and several related, work-focused questions. The photos and questions activate learners' prior knowledge by getting them to think and talk about the unit topic. The **Performance Preview**, which gives an overview of all the skills in the unit, helps teachers set goals and purposes for the unit. Optionally, teachers may want to examine the Performance Preview with learners before they begin the unit.

Getting Started

An initial **Team Work** activity presents key work skills, concepts, and language introduced in the unit. It consists of active critical thinking and peer teaching to activate the use of the new language and to preview the content

To the Teacher

of the unit. A **Partner Work** or **Practice the Dialog** activity encourages learners to use the new language in communicative ways. A culminating class or group **Survey** encourages learners to relate the new language to themselves and their workplaces or career interests.

Talk About It

This page provides opportunities for spoken communication. **Practice the Dialog** provides a model for conversation. **Partner Work** presents a personalized **On Your Job** activity that allows learners to use the model in Practice the Dialog to talk about their own workplace experiences.

Useful Language The **Useful Language** box contains related words, phrases, and expressions for learners to use as they complete Partner Work.

ASAP PROJECT The **ASAP Project** is a long-term project learners complete over the course of the unit. Learners create items such as files of human resources forms, lists of interview questions, and work schedules that they can use outside of the classroom.

Keep Talking

The Keep Talking page contains additional conversation models and speaking tasks. It also includes the **Personal Dictionary** feature. This feature allows learners to record the language relevant to the unit topic that they need to do their jobs. Because each learner's job is different, this personalized resource enables learners to focus on the language that is most useful to them. In addition, learners can use this feature in conjunction with Steck-Vaughn's *Workforce Writing Dictionary* to create a completely customized lexicon of key words and phrases they need to know.

Listening

The Listening page develops SCANS-based listening skills. Tasks include listening for greetings, names of places, directions, instructions, and times.

All the activities develop the skill of **focused listening.** Learners learn to recognize the information they need and to listen selectively for only that information. They do not have to understand every word; rather, they have to filter out everything except the relevant information. This essential skill is used by native speakers of all languages.

Many of the activities involve **multi-task listening**. In these activities, called **Listen Again** and **Listen Once More**, learners listen to the same selection several times and complete a different task each time. First they might listen for the main idea. They might listen again for specific information. They might listen a third time in order to draw conclusions or make inferences.

Culminating discussion questions allow learners to relate the information they have heard to their own needs and interests.

A complete Listening Transcript for all dialogs recorded on the Audiocassettes but not appearing directly on the Student Book pages is at the back of the Student Book and Teacher's Edition. All the selections are recorded on the Audiocassettes.

Grammar

Grammar, a two-page spread, presents key grammatical structures that complement the unit competencies. Language boxes show the new language in a clear, simple format that allows learners to make generalizations about the new language. Oral and written exercises provide contextualized reinforcement relevant to the workplace.

Reading and Writing

Reading selections, such as excerpts from instruction manuals, job evaluations, and timecards, focus on items learners encounter at work. Exercises and discussion questions develop reading skills and help learners relate the content of the selections to their workplaces or career interests.

The writing tasks, often related to the reading selection, help learners develop writing skills, such as completing job applications, writing to-do lists, and writing schedules.

Extension

The Extension page enriches the previous instruction. As in other sections, realia is used extensively. Oral and written exercises help learners master the additional skills, language, and concepts, and relate them to their workplaces and career interests.

CultureNotes **Culture Notes**, a feature that appears on each Extension page, sparks lively, engaging discussion. Topics include asking for directions, using machines, using employee handbooks, and exchanging greetings.

Performance Check

The two-page Performance Check allows teachers and learners to track learners' progress and to meet the learner verification needs of schools, companies, or programs. All work skills are tested in the same manner they are presented in the units; so, formats are familiar and non-threatening, and success is built in. The **Performance Review** at the end of each test alerts teachers and learners to the work skills that are being evaluated. The check-off boxes allow learners to track their success and gain a sense of accomplishment and satisfaction. Finally, a culminating discussion allows learners to relate their new skills to their development as effective workers.

Teaching Techniques

Make Your Classroom Mirror the Workplace

Help learners develop workplace skills

by setting up your classroom to mirror a workplace. Use any of these suggestions.

◆ Establish policies on lateness and absence similar to those a business might have.

◆ Provide learners with a daily agenda of the activities they will complete that day, including partner work and small group assignments. Go over the agenda with learners at the beginning and end of class.

◆ With learner input, establish a list of goals for the class. Goals can include speaking, reading, and writing English every day; using effective teamwork skills; or learning ten new vocabulary words each day. Go over the goals with learners at regular intervals.

◆ Assign students regular jobs and responsibilities, such as arranging the chairs in a circle, setting up the overhead projector, or making copies for the class.

Presenting a Unit Opener

The unit opener sets the stage for the unit. Use the photos and questions to encourage learners to:

◆ Speculate about what the unit might cover.

◆ Activate prior knowledge.

◆ Relate what they see in the photos to their own work environments.

Peer Teaching

Because each adult learner brings rich life experience to the classroom, *English ASAP* is designed to help you use each learner's expertise as a resource for peer teaching.

Here are some practical strategies for peer teaching:

◆ Have learners work in pairs/small groups to clarify new language concepts for each other.

◆ If a learner possesses a particular work skill, appoint that learner as "class consultant" in that area and have learners direct queries to that individual.

◆ Set up a reference area in a corner of your classroom. Include dictionaries, career books, and other books your learners will find useful.

Partner Work and Team Work

The abundance of Partner Work and Team Work activities in *English ASAP* serves the dual purposes of developing learners' communicative competence and providing learners with experience using key SCANS interpersonal skills, such as working in teams, teaching others, leading, negotiating, and working well with people from culturally diverse backgrounds. To take full advantage of these activities, follow these suggestions.

◆ Whenever students work in groups, appoint, or have students select, a leader.

◆ Use multiple groupings. Have learners work with different partners and teams, just as workers do in the workplace. For different activities, you might group learners according to language ability, skill, or learner interest.

◆ Make sure learners understand that everyone on the team is responsible for the team's work.

◆ At the end of each activity, have teams report the results to the class.

◆ Discuss with learners their teamwork skills and talk about ways teams can work together effectively. They can discuss how to clarify roles and responsibilities, resolve disagreements effectively, communicate openly, and make decisions together.

Purpose Statement

Each page after the unit opener begins with a brief purpose statement that summarizes the work skills presented on that page. When learners first begin working on a page, focus their attention on the purpose statement and help them read it. Ask them what the page will be about. Discuss with the class why the skill is important. Ask learners to talk about their prior knowledge of the skill. Finally, show learners how using the skill will help them become more effective on their jobs.

Survey

The **Survey** on each **Getting Started** page helps learners relate the new language and skills to their own lives. Before learners begin the activity, help them create questions they'll need to ask. Assist them in deciding how they'll record their answers. You may need to model taking notes, using tally marks, and other simple ways to record information. Assist learners in setting a time limit before they begin. Remember to allow learners to move about the room as they complete the activity.

Many Survey results can be summarized in a bar graph or pie chart.

◆ A bar graph uses bars to represent numbers. Bar graphs have two scales, a vertical scale and a horizontal scale. For example, to graph the number of learners who get paid by check versus those paid by direct deposit, the vertical scale can represent numbers of students, such as 2, 4, 6, 8, etc. The horizontal scale can consist of two bars. One bar represents the number of learners paid by check. The other bar represents the number of learners paid by direct deposit. The two bars can be different colors to set them apart. Bars should be the same width.

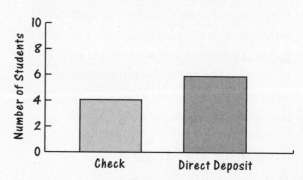

To the Teacher

◆ A pie chart shows the parts that make up a whole set of facts. Each part of the pie is a percentage of the whole. For example, a pie chart might show 40% of learners are paid by check and 60% are paid by direct deposit.

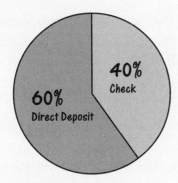

Presenting a Dialog

To present a dialog, follow these suggested steps:

◆ Play the tape or say the dialog aloud two or more times. Ask one or two simple questions to make sure learners understand.

◆ Say the dialog aloud line-by-line for learners to repeat chorally, by rows, and then individually.

◆ Have learners say or read the dialog together in pairs.

◆ Have several pairs say or read the dialog aloud for the class.

Presenting the Personal Dictionary

The Personal Dictionary enables learners to focus on the vocabulary in each unit that is relevant to their particular jobs. To use this feature, have learners work in teams to brainstorm vocabulary words they might put in their dictionaries. Have team reporters share their ideas with the class. Then allow learners a few minutes to add to their dictionaries. Remind students to continue adding words throughout the unit.

For further vocabulary development, learners can enter the words from their Personal Dictionary into their *Workforce Writing Dictionaries.*

To the Teacher

Presenting a Listening Activity

Use any of these suggestions:

◆ To activate learners' prior knowledge, have them look at the illustrations, if any, and say as much as they can about them. Encourage them to make inferences about the content of the listening selection.

◆ Have learners read the directions. To encourage them to focus their listening, have them read the questions before they listen so that they know exactly what to listen for.

◆ Play the tape or read the Listening Transcript aloud as learners complete the activity. Rewind the tape and play it again as necessary.

◆ Help learners check their work.

In multi-task listening, remind learners that they will listen to the same passage several times and answer different questions each time. After learners complete a section, have them check their own or each others' work before you rewind the tape and proceed to the next questions.

Presenting a Tip

Tip A variety of tips throughout each unit present valuable advice on how to be a successful employee and/or language learner. To present a tip, help learners read the tip. Discuss it with them. Ask them how it will help them. For certain tips, such as those in which learners make lists, you may want to allow learners time to start the activity.

Presenting a Discussion

English ASAP provides a variety of whole-class and team discussions. Always encourage students to state their ideas and respond appropriately to other learners' comments. At the end of each discussion, have team reporters summarize their team's ideas and/or help the class come to a consensus about the topic.

Prereading

To help learners read the selections with ease and success, establish a purpose for reading and call on learners' prior knowledge to make inferences about the reading. Use any of these techniques:

◆ Have learners look over and describe any photographs, realia, and/or illustrations. Ask them to use the illustrations to say what they think the selection might be about.

◆ Have learners read the title and any heads or sub-heads. Ask them what kind of information they think is in the selection and how it might be organized. Ask them where they might encounter such information outside of class and why they would want to read it.

◆ To help learners focus their reading, have them review the comprehension activities before they read the selection. Ask them what kind of information they think they will find out when they read. Restate their ideas and/or write them on the board in acceptable English.

◆ Remind learners that they do not have to know all the words in order to understand the selection.

Evaluation

To use the Performance Check pages successfully, follow these suggested procedures:
Before and during each evaluation, create a relaxed, affirming atmosphere. Chat with the learners for a few minutes and review the material. When you and the learners are ready, have learners read the directions and look over each exercise before they complete it. If at any time you sense that learners are becoming frustrated, stop to provide additional review. Resume when learners are ready. The evaluation formats follow two basic patterns:

1. **Speaking** competencies are checked in the format used to present them in the unit. Have learners read the instructions. Make sure learners know what to do. Then have learners complete the evaluation in one of these ways:

Self- and Peer Evaluation: Have learners complete the spoken activity in pairs. Learners in each pair evaluate themselves and/or each other and report the results to you.

Teacher/Pair Evaluation: Have pairs complete the activity as you observe and evaluate their work. Begin with the most proficient learners. As other learners who are ready to be evaluated wait, have them practice in pairs. Learners who complete the evaluation successfully can peer-teach those who are waiting or those who need additional review.

Teacher/Individual Evaluation: Have individuals complete the activity with you as their partner. Follow the procedures in Teacher/Pair Evaluation.

2. **Listening, reading,** and **writing** competencies are also all checked in the same format used to present them in the unit. When learners are ready to begin, have them read the instructions. Demonstrate the first item and have learners complete the activity. In Listening activities, play the tape or read the Listening Transcript aloud two or more times. Then have learners check their work. Provide any review needed, and have learners try the activity again.

When learners demonstrate mastery of a skill to your satisfaction, have them record their success by checking the appropriate box in the Performance Review. The Teacher's Edition also contains charts for you to reproduce to keep track of individual and class progress.

To the Teacher

Steck-Vaughn

English ASAP

Connecting English to the Workplace

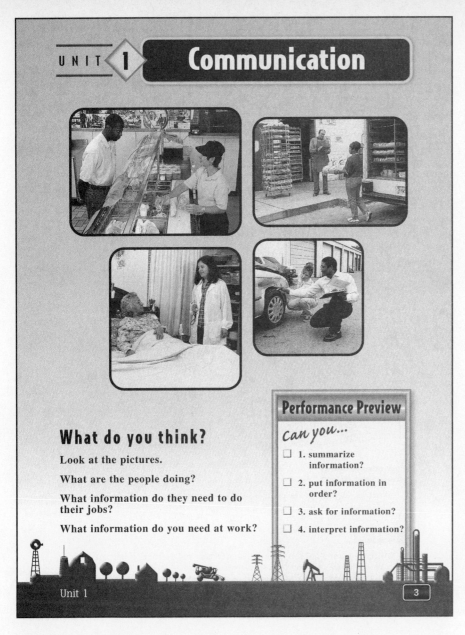

UNIT 1 — Communication

What do you think?

Look at the pictures.

What are the people doing?

What information do they need to do their jobs?

What information do you need at work?

Performance Preview

Can you...

☐ 1. summarize information?

☐ 2. put information in order?

☐ 3. ask for information?

☐ 4. interpret information?

Unit 1

3

Unit 1 Overview

—SCANS Competencies—

★ Acquire and evaluate information

★ Interpret and communicate information

★ Organize information

★ Improve systems

Workforce Skills

● Summarize information

● Put information in order

● Ask for information

● Interpret information

Materials

● A daily organizer; taco ingredients or picture cards of taco ingredients; picture cards of an air filter, faucet, and damaged carpet; realia or picture cards of a starched dress shirt and/or a dress shirt and spray starch.

● Telephone message forms, restaurant guest checks, a self-stick notepad, and a supply request form; a variety of sample forms, such as work orders and suggestion cards

Unit Warm-Up

To get the learners thinking about the unit topic (acquiring and organizing information), role-play a search for information, such as the last day of class. Search in vain through your briefcase. Repeat using an organizer. Flip immediately to the correct page. Ask learners to contrast.

★　　★　　★　　★　　★

WORKFORCE SKILLS (page 3)

Summarize information

Ask for information

PREPARATION

Explain that people in different occupations require different information to do their jobs. Ask learners how the information that doctors need is different from the information that auto mechanics need.

PRESENTATION

1. Focus attention on the photographs. Ask learners to speculate what the unit might be about. Write their ideas on the board and/or restate them in acceptable English.

2. Have learners talk about the photographs. Have them identify the situations and say what questions they think the people are asking and answering.

3. Help learners read the questions. Discuss the questions with the class.

4. You may want to use the Performance Preview to provide learners with an overview of the skills in the unit. Have students read the list of skills and discuss what they will learn in the unit.

FOLLOW-UP

Information Please: Ask each learner to choose one of the employees shown on this page. Then have learners think of a question that employee might have about how to do his or her job. As each learner, in turn, states his or her question, other learners identify the employee who would ask it.

♦ Divide the class into four teams and assign each a photograph on the page. Ask them to imagine something has come up that the employee does not know how to deal with. Have the teams brainstorm ways employees could get additional information to do the job. Have team reporters summarize ideas for the class.

WORKBOOK

Unit 1, Exercises 1A–1B

★ ★ ★ ★ ★

Teaching Note

Use this page to introduce the new language in this unit. Whenever possible, encourage peer teaching. Supply any new language the learners need.

Culture Note

Help learners make a list of phrases they can use when they don't understand something. For example, students can say, "Could you please repeat that," "Would you mind explaining that," or "Could you say that again more slowly, please?"

Getting Started — Asking for information

TEAM WORK

Match the question with the situation. Can you think of other questions?

a. How do I fill out a work order?
b. Who should I call to fix the ceiling?
c. Where do I put these movies?
d. When should I pour the concrete?

PARTNER WORK

What do you need to find out today at your workplace or school?
Take turns saying your questions.

SURVEY

Work with 2 or 3 learners. Make a list of 5 common questions people ask at your workplace or school. Ask learners in other groups whether they ask or hear those questions at work or school. How many learners hear each question?

4

Unit 1

PREPARATION

To present or review **ceiling** and **concrete,** identify these items in your classroom.

PRESENTATION

1. Have learners read and discuss the Purpose Statement. For more information, see "Purpose Statement" on page viii.

2. Focus attention on the illustrations. Encourage learners to say as much as they can about them. Write their ideas on the board and/or restate them in acceptable English.

3. Have teams read the Team Work instructions. Make sure each team knows what to do. Remind the teams that they are responsible for making sure that each member understands the new language. Then have teams complete the activity. If learners need help, encourage them to consult other teams. Have team reporters share their answers with the class.

4. Have partners read the Partner Work instructions. Make sure partners know what to do. Then have partners complete the activity. Have learners switch partners and repeat the activity. Supply any language needed. Have one or two pairs present their questions to the class.

5. Have teams read the Survey instructions. Make sure everyone knows what to do. Then have teams complete the activity. Have teams share their answers with the class. For more information, see "Survey" on page viii.

FOLLOW-UP

Graph: Ask each team to create a bar graph to show the results of the survey. The horizontal axis should show the 5 common questions people ask; the vertical axis, the number of learners who have heard each question. Post the graphs in the classroom. For more information, see "Survey" on page viii.

♦ Discuss with learners the questions they ask and answer at work. What are the most difficult questions?

WORKBOOK

Unit 1, Exercises 2A–2B

Talk About It

Asking for the information that you need

PRACTICE THE DIALOG

A I'd like to have these shirts laundered.

B Starch or no starch?

A Starch in two of them and no starch in one, please.

B Which ones get starch?

A These two white dress shirts.

B The two white dress shirts get starch. When do you want them? Is Tuesday OK?

A Sure, Tuesday's fine.

Tip
To show that you understand, repeat bosses' and customers' instructions.

Useful Language

Who...?   When...?
What...?   Why...?
Where...?   How...?

PARTNER WORK

You work in these places. What information do you need to know? Take turns asking each other questions. Use the dialog and the Useful Language above.

1. Best Plumbing Co.   **2.** Andy's Car Repairs   **3.** Speedy Delivery Service

ASAP PROJECT

Work as a team. Make a list of ways to find out about job openings in your area. Think about resources such as newspaper ads, job boards, local employment offices, and so on. Share your list with the class.

Unit 1

5

ASAP PROJECT

Have learners read the instructions. Discuss the project and its purpose with learners. Make sure that everyone understands. Help learners assign themselves to teams based upon their knowledge, skills, interests, or other personal strengths. Have each team select a leader, and have the team leaders or the whole class select an overall project leader. Throughout the rest of the unit, allow time for learners to work on the project. Have the teams agree on a deadline when the project will be finished. For more information, see "ASAP Project" on page vi.

PREPARATION

Use realia or picture cards to present or review: shirts, laundered, starch, and dress shirts.

PRESENTATION

1. Have learners read and discuss the Purpose Statement. For more information, see "Purpose Statement" on page viii.

 2. Focus attention on the photograph. Encourage learners to say as much as they can about it. Have them ask questions about the situation. Write their ideas on the board and/or express them in acceptable English. Then present the dialog. See "Presenting a Dialog" on page ix.

3. Have partners read the Partner Work instructions. Focus attention on the Useful Language box. Help learners read the words. If necessary, model pronunciation. Then have learners complete the activity. Have learners switch partners and repeat the activity. Have one or two pairs present their dialogs to the class.

Tip Have learners read the Tip independently. Have learners discuss how the advice will help them. For more information, see "Presenting a Tip" on page ix.

FOLLOW-UP

Dialogs: Have learners work in pairs. One partner should identify a task at work or at home. The other should ask questions about it using the words in

Useful Language, then repeat each answer after it is given. Have partners switch roles and repeat the activity. Have several pairs present their dialogs to the class.

♦ Have partners write their dialogs.

WORKBOOK

Unit 1, Exercises 3A–3B

★   ★   ★   ★   ★

Language Note

*Help learners identify words that indicate sequence of events. First encourage them to find sequence words on the page. (**first, next,** and **then**) Then have them add others, such as **before** and **after**. Explain that these words help order information. Have volunteers use the words to describe the steps in tasks such as putting in a lawn, changing a bed, or filing a stack of papers.*

Personal Dictionary

Have learners add the words in their Personal Dictionary to their *Workforce Writing Dictionary*. For more information, see "Workforce Writing Dictionary" on page v.

Keep Talking — Putting information in order

PRACTICE THE DIALOG

A How do I make a taco?

B Start with the taco shells on this shelf. Then add the meat.

A OK, what's next?

B Next you put on the refrigerated items. The ingredients are arranged in the order that you should put them on the taco. Lettuce first, then tomatoes, onions, and cheese.

PARTNER WORK

Are there tasks at your workplace or school that you have to do in a particular order? Take turns explaining to your partner the steps you follow.

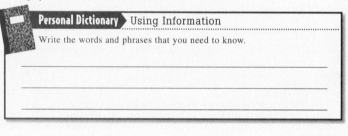
Personal Dictionary — Using Information

Write the words and phrases that you need to know.

_____

_____

_____

6   Unit 1

PREPARATION

1. Use realia or pictures to present or review **taco, taco shells,** and taco ingredients.

2. Describe how to prepare a particular food. Write the sequencing words on the board as you use them.

PRESENTATION

1. Have learners read the Purpose Statement. For more information, see "Purpose Statement" on page viii.

 2. Focus attention on the illustration. Have learners say as much as they can about it. Have them identify the food items they see. Write their ideas on the board and/or restate them in acceptable English. Then present the dialog. See "Presenting a Dialog" on page ix.

3. Have partners read the Partner Work instructions. Make sure each partner knows what to do. If necessary, model the activity. Then have partners complete the activity. Ask several learners to share descriptions of tasks with the class.

4. Have learners read the Personal Dictionary instructions. Then use the Personal Dictionary procedures on page ix. Remind learners to continue to add words to their dictionaries throughout the unit.

FOLLOW-UP

Organizing Information: Have partners write each ingredient used to make a taco on a separate slip of paper. Have pairs shuffle the papers and exchange them with another pair. Have pairs order the slips to show the steps in which ingredients are put on a taco. Have one or two pairs read their slips, in order, to the class.

♦ Choose a task, such as unpacking a box and placing the contents on a shelf. Write each step on a separate slip of paper. Shuffle the papers and have teams put the steps in order. Check each team's work.

WORKBOOK

Unit 1, Exercises 4A–4B

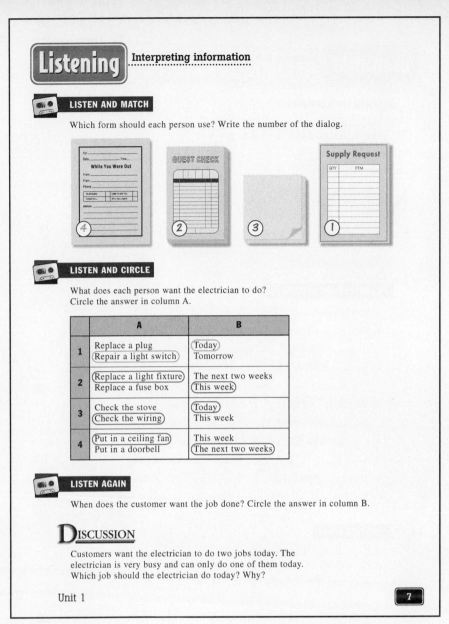

Listening — Interpreting information

LISTEN AND MATCH

Which form should each person use? Write the number of the dialog.

LISTEN AND CIRCLE

What does each person want the electrician to do?
Circle the answer in column A.

	A	B
1	Replace a plug / (Repair a light switch)	(Today) / Tomorrow
2	(Replace a light fixture) / Replace a fuse box	The next two weeks / (This week)
3	Check the stove / (Check the wiring)	(Today) / This week
4	(Put in a ceiling fan) / Put in a doorbell	This week / (The next two weeks)

LISTEN AGAIN

When does the customer want the job done? Circle the answer in column B.

DISCUSSION

Customers want the electrician to do two jobs today. The electrician is very busy and can only do one of them today. Which job should the electrician do today? Why?

Unit 1　　　　7

PREPARATION

1. To present or review plug, switch, fixture, wiring, and ceiling fan, point out these objects in the classroom or use picture cards. Explain that an electrician is a person who works with these items.

2. Display real or enlarged copies of a telephone message form, guest check, self-stick notepad, and supply request form. Discuss the type of information that is appropriate for each. Ask learners who have used these forms to explain what they've used them for.

PRESENTATION

1. Have learners read and discuss the Purpose Statement. For more information, see "Purpose Statement" on page viii.

 2. Have learners read the Listen and Match instructions. Then have them look at the forms.

Make sure that everyone understands the instructions. Then play the tape or read the Listening Transcript aloud two or more times as learners complete the activity. Have learners check their work. For more information, see "Presenting a Listening Activity" on page ix.

 3. Have learners read the Listen and Circle instructions. Then follow the procedures in 2.

 4. Have learners read the Listen Again instructions. Then follow the procedures in 2.

5. Have learners read the Discussion instructions. Make sure everyone knows what to do. Then have learners work in teams to discuss what the electrician should do. Have team reporters share their teams' answers with the class.

FOLLOW-UP

Form and Function: Bring in forms from local businesses, such as work orders, purchase orders, customer surveys, inventory charts, etc. Give each team a different form. Have each team suggest businesses that might use it. Have teams share their ideas with the class.

◆ Give each pair of learners two blank telephone message forms. One partner should answer the phone and take a message for a colleague at work or at school. The caller should request that a specific task be done on a specific day. Then have partners switch roles and repeat. Ask several learners to read their message to the class.

WORKBOOK

Unit 1, Exercise 5

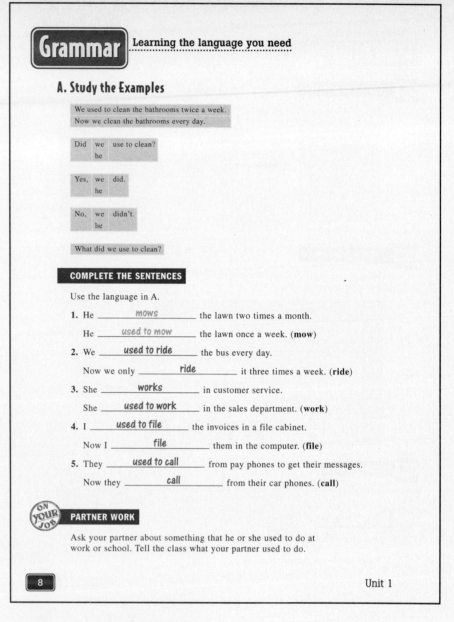

Grammar · Learning the language you need

A. Study the Examples

We used to clean the bathrooms twice a week.
Now we clean the bathrooms every day.

| Did | we | use to clean? |
| | he | |

| Yes, | we | did. |
| | he | |

| No, | we | didn't. |
| | he | |

What did we use to clean?

COMPLETE THE SENTENCES

Use the language in A.

1. He _____ *mows* _____ the lawn two times a month.

   He _____ *used to mow* _____ the lawn once a week. (**mow**)

2. We _____ *used to ride* _____ the bus every day.

   Now we only _____ *ride* _____ it three times a week. (**ride**)

3. She _____ *works* _____ in customer service.

   She _____ *used to work* _____ in the sales department. (**work**)

4. I _____ *used to file* _____ the invoices in a file cabinet.

   Now I _____ *file* _____ them in the computer. (**file**)

5. They _____ *used to call* _____ from pay phones to get their messages.

   Now they _____ *call* _____ from their car phones. (**call**)

PARTNER WORK

Ask your partner about something that he or she used to do at work or school. Tell the class what your partner used to do.

8   Unit 1

PREPARATION

Review the language in the grammar boxes with learners before they open their books, if necessary. Use realia to present or review a diagram. Use picture cards or pantomime to present or review delivery.

PRESENTATION

1. Have learners read and discuss the Purpose Statement. For more information, see "Purpose Statement" on page viii.

2. Have learners read the grammar boxes in A. Have learners use the language in the boxes to say as many sentences as possible. Tell learners that they can use the grammar boxes throughout the unit to review or check sentence structures.

3. Have learners read the instructions for Complete the Sentences. If necessary, model the first item. Allow learners to complete the activity. Have learners check each other's work in pairs. Have a different learner read each sentence aloud as the rest of the class checks their answers.

4. Have learners read the Partner Work instructions. Make sure each partner knows what to do. Then have partners complete the activity. Ask partners to share with the class what they found out about each other.

8   English ASAP

B. Study the Examples

> I got the tools while Fred was looking at the diagram.
> While Fred was looking at the diagram, I got the tools.

COMPLETE THE SENTENCES

Use the language in B.

1. Don and Lee _____were taking_____ (**take**) the inventory when

   we _____walked_____ (**walk**) into the stock room.

2. When the new cashier _____arrived_____ (**arrive**),

   Mr. Mars _____was talking_____ (**talk**) to a customer.

3. While Elsa _____was filling_____ (**fill**) the bucket with water,

   Suzy _____got_____ (**got**) the mop.

4. While I _____was fixing_____ (**fix**) the sink,

   the toilet _____broke_____ (**break**).

C. Study the Examples

I	made a delivery this morning.
You	counted the bread and rolls last night.
He	
She	
We	
They	

drive	drove
have	had
make	made
take	took

COMPLETE THE SENTENCES

Use the language in C.

We _____made_____ (**make**) 12 bakery deliveries yesterday. Sarah and

I _____took_____ (**take**) the new truck to the south side to deliver some

cakes. Pedro _____used_____ (**use**) the old truck to take some cookies

downtown. He _____had_____ (**have**) three or four deliveries in that

area. Amanda _____drove_____ (**drive**) the van to the Grand Hotel.

She _____delivered_____ (**deliver**) some rolls there.

Unit 1   9

---

5. Focus attention on the grammar box in B. Follow the procedures in 2.

6. Have learners read the instructions for Complete the Sentences. Then follow the procedures in 3.

7. Focus attention on the grammar boxes in C. Follow the procedures in 2.

8. Have learners read the instructions for Complete the Sentences. Then follow the procedures in 3.

FOLLOW-UP

Then and Now: Have partners write each verb in parentheses on pages 8 and 9 on a separate slip of paper. Have partners take turns drawing slips of paper and using the verb to talk about something they did in the past or do now. Ask several pairs to share their "then and now" statements with the class.

♦ Ask learners to write their "then and now" sentences. Check learners' work.

WORKBOOK

Unit 1, Exercises 6A–6C

BLACKLINE MASTERS

Blackline Master: Unit 1

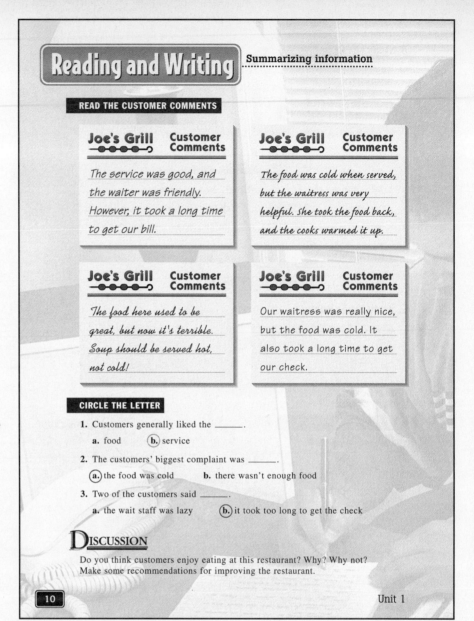

Teaching Note

Explain that a summary is a shortened restatement of the main idea(s) of a sentence, paragraph, or article. Suggest that when learners summarize they should eliminate unimportant or repeated ideas and combine similar ideas into one general statement. Help learners summarize a short paragraph as an example.

PREPARATION

1. Use a picture of a restaurant, or role-play a food server waiting on customers to present or review check, bill, waitress, waiter, wait staff, and service.

2. Explain that summarize means "to restate an idea in fewer words, such as restating a sentence as a phrase." Give an example.

PRESENTATION

1. Have learners read and discuss the Purpose Statement. For more information, see "Purpose Statement" on page viii.

2. Have learners preview the customer comment cards before they read. See "Prereading" on page x. Encourage learners to say everything they can

about the cards. Write their ideas on the board and/or restate them in acceptable English. Then have them read the cards independently.

3. Have learners read the instructions for Circle the Letter. Make sure everyone knows what to do. Then have learners complete the activity independently. Have learners review each other's work in pairs. Ask several learners to share their answers with the class while the rest of the class checks their work.

4. Have learners read the Discussion instructions. Make sure everyone knows what to do. Then have learners work in teams to discuss whether customers enjoy the restaurant and how it can be improved. Have team reporters share their ideas with the class.

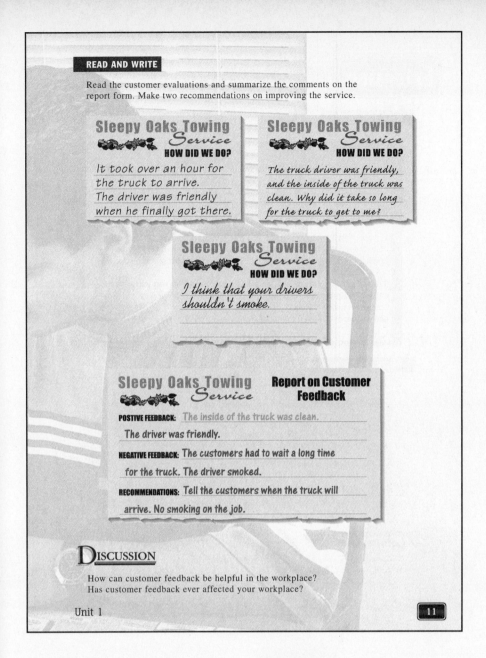

Read the customer evaluations and summarize the comments on the report form. Make two recommendations on improving the service.

Sleepy Oaks Towing
Service
HOW DID WE DO?

It took over an hour for the truck to arrive. The driver was friendly when he finally got there.

Sleepy Oaks Towing
Service
HOW DID WE DO?

The truck driver was friendly, and the inside of the truck was clean. Why did it take so long for the truck to get to me?

Sleepy Oaks Towing
Service
HOW DID WE DO?

I think that your drivers shouldn't smoke.

Sleepy Oaks Towing
Service

Report on Customer Feedback

POSITIVE FEEDBACK: The inside of the truck was clean. The driver was friendly.

NEGATIVE FEEDBACK: The customers had to wait a long time for the truck. The driver smoked.

RECOMMENDATIONS: Tell the customers when the truck will arrive. No smoking on the job.

DISCUSSION

How can customer feedback be helpful in the workplace? Has customer feedback ever affected your workplace?

Unit 1

11

5. Have learners preview the customer evaluation forms before they read. See "Prereading" on page x. Encourage learners to say everything they can about the forms. Write their ideas on the board and/or restate them in acceptable English. Then have them read the forms independently.

6. Have learners read the instructions for Read and Write. Model the activity if necessary. Then have learners complete the activity independently. Have several learners read their feedback and suggestions aloud.

7. Have learners read the Discussion instructions. Make sure everyone knows what to do. Then have learners work in teams to answer the questions. Have team reporters summarize their discussions for the class.

FOLLOW-UP

Improve Service: Have learners work in teams. Ask each team to choose a local business they use regularly, such as a supermarket, convenience store, or bus company. Ask each team to come up with a list of ways the business can improve customer service. Have teams share their lists with the class.

♦ Have teams summarize their recommendations. Ask team reporters to read the summaries to the class.

WORKBOOK

Unit 1, Exercises 7A–7B

Extension — Analyzing information

READ THE ARTICLE

Happy Home Apartments

Guidelines for Maintenance Workers

In order to maintain a comfortable and safe residence, Happy Home Apartments requires that all maintenance crews follow these guidelines.

1. Before entering any apartment, first knock loudly on the door. After you wait for the residents to open the door, you can enter the apartment with the key.
2. While you are in the apartment, put a notice on the door saying that you are working in the apartment.
3. When you finish the repairs, leave a note to the residents that you were in their apartment during the day. The note should include the date and time of your repairs.
4. If you need to move furniture to make a repair, give the residents 24 hours' notice.

WRITE THE NUMBER

What should they do? Write the number of the rule.

___2___ 1. Min Lee has entered an apartment. She will be in the apartment putting up wallpaper for several hours.

___3___ 2. Bob has been in an apartment checking the air filters. He stayed for only ten minutes, and now he's ready to leave.

___1___ 3. Joseph isn't sure if the residents of apartment 9 are home. He needs to enter the apartment to repair a broken faucet.

___4___ 4. Alex is going to replace some damaged carpet in apartment 3. He needs to move the furniture before he can start his job.

 Culture Notes

You need to ask your boss a question, but you can't find her. What do you do?

12   Unit 1

PREPARATION

Use picture cards and/or explanation to teach or review **air filter, faucet,** and **damaged carpet.**

PRESENTATION

1. Have learners read and discuss the Purpose Statement. For more information, see "Purpose Statement" on page viii.

2. Have learners preview the information in the guidelines. Encourage them to say everything they can about the guidelines. Write their ideas on the board and/or restate them in acceptable English. Then have learners read the guidelines independently.

3. Have learners read the instructions for Write the Number. If necessary, model the first item. Allow learners to complete the activity. Ask several learners to read their answers aloud while the rest of the class checks their work.

4. Have learners read Culture Notes and talk over their responses in teams. Have team reporters share their ideas with the class. For more information, see "Culture Notes" on page vii.

FOLLOW-UP

The Perfect Workplace: Assign each team a workplace, such as a restaurant, auto repair shop, or video rental store. Have teams write guidelines for the workers. If necessary, provide examples, such as: Respect fellow employees. Have team reporters share guidelines with the class. Post them in the classroom.

♦ Have teams compare all of the guidelines and make a list of general guidelines that apply to all workplaces. Have teams compare their lists.

WORKBOOK

Unit 1, Exercise 8

Performance Check

How well can you use the skills in this unit?

Complete the activities. Go over your work with a partner or your teacher. Then complete the Performance Review on page 14.

SKILL 1 **SUMMARIZE INFORMATION**

Complete the report.

Bright & Shiny CLEANERS

Cleaning Crew Evaluation

The cleaning was excellent, but the crew arrived an hour late. I prefer prompt service.

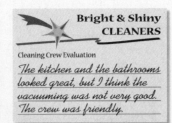

Bright & Shiny CLEANERS

Cleaning Crew Evaluation

The kitchen and the bathrooms looked great, but I think the vacuuming was not very good. The crew was friendly.

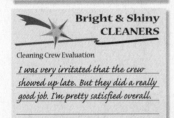

Bright & Shiny CLEANERS

Cleaning Crew Evaluation

I was very irritated that the crew showed up late. But they did a really good job. I'm pretty satisfied overall.

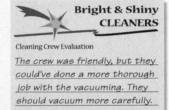

Bright & Shiny CLEANERS

Cleaning Crew Evaluation

The crew was friendly, but they could've done a more thorough job with the vacuuming. They should vacuum more carefully.

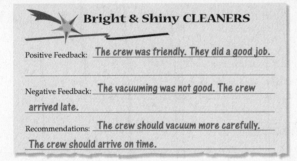

Bright & Shiny CLEANERS

Positive Feedback: The crew was friendly. They did a good job.

Negative Feedback: The vacuuming was not good. The crew arrived late.

Recommendations: The crew should vacuum more carefully. The crew should arrive on time.

Unit 1

13

PRESENTATION

Use any of the procedures in "Evaluation," page x, with pages 13 and 14. Record individuals' results on the Unit 1 Individual Competency Chart. Record the class's results on the Class Cumulative Competency Chart.

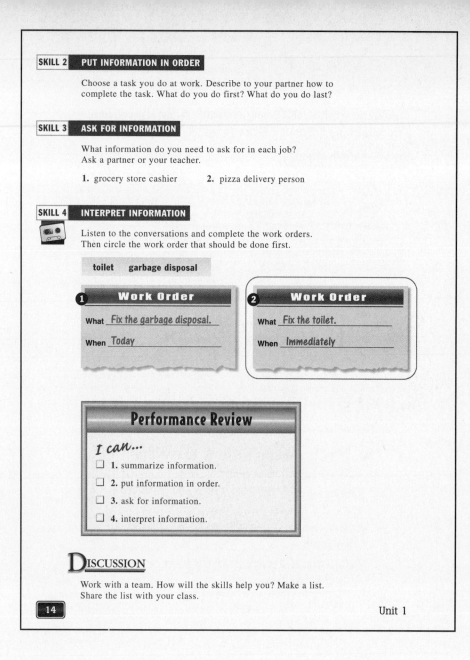

SKILL 2 PUT INFORMATION IN ORDER

Choose a task you do at work. Describe to your partner how to complete the task. What do you do first? What do you do last?

SKILL 3 ASK FOR INFORMATION

What information do you need to ask for in each job?
Ask a partner or your teacher.

1. grocery store cashier   2. pizza delivery person

SKILL 4 INTERPRET INFORMATION

Listen to the conversations and complete the work orders.
Then circle the work order that should be done first.

toilet   garbage disposal

1 Work Order

What Fix the garbage disposal.

When Today

2 Work Order

What Fix the toilet.

When Immediately

Performance Review

I can...

☐ 1. summarize information.

☐ 2. put information in order.

☐ 3. ask for information.

☐ 4. interpret information.

DISCUSSION

Work with a team. How will the skills help you? Make a list.
Share the list with your class.

14   Unit 1

PRESENTATION

Follow the instructions on page 13.

INFORMAL WORKPLACE-SPECIFIC ASSESSMENT

Have learners make lists of information they would like to have about their workplaces. Have them state questions they could ask to get the information they want.

WORKBOOK

Unit 1, Exercise 9

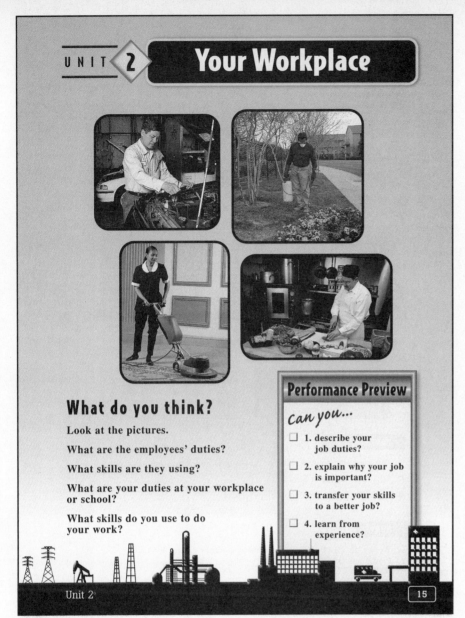

What do you think?

Look at the pictures.

What are the employees' duties?

What skills are they using?

What are your duties at your workplace or school?

What skills do you use to do your work?

Performance Preview

can you...

☐ 1. describe your job duties?

☐ 2. explain why your job is important?

☐ 3. transfer your skills to a better job?

☐ 4. learn from experience?

Unit 2   15

Unit 2 Overview
—SCANS Competencies—

★ Interpret and communicate information

★ Understand organizational systems

★ Monitor and correct performance

★ Work on teams

Workforce Skills

● Describe your job duties

● Explain why your job is important

● Transfer your skills to a better job

● Learn from experience

Materials

● Picture cards of people at work, including employees in a restaurant and workers at a loading dock

● Picture cards or realia to present cashier, timer, gas gauge, weather report, groundskeeper, driver's license, lawn, shrubs, carpenter, hardware, and bookkeeper

● Help-wanted ads

Unit Warm-Up

To get the learners thinking about the unit topic (describing their jobs and transferring their skills to a better job), show learners picture cards of people at work. Ask learners to describe each job.

★　　★　　★　　★　　★

WORKFORCE SKILLS (page 15)

Explain why your job is important

★　　★　　★　　★　　★

PREPARATION

Ask learners to describe your job as a teacher. List your **duties** or responsibilities on the board as learners mention them. Supply any additional language learners need.

PRESENTATION

1. Focus attention on the photographs. Ask learners to speculate what the unit might be about. Write their ideas on the board and/or restate them in acceptable English.

2. Have learners talk about the photographs. Ask them what the workers are doing and what type of company employs each of them.

3. Help learners read the questions. Discuss the questions with the class.

4. You may want to use the Performance Preview to provide learners with an overview of the skills in the unit. Have learners read the list of skills and discuss what they will learn in the unit.

FOLLOW-UP

Mystery Jobs: Divide the class into teams. Have each team choose a job. Ask teams to say 3 key words that describe that job without revealing the job. For example, for **baggage handler,** learners might list **travel, suitcase,** and **lift.** The other teams figure out the job and name the employee's duties.

♦ Have teams use the key words in sentences to describe the job. Have team reporters read the sentences to the class.

WORKBOOK

Unit 2, Exercises 1A–1B

★   ★   ★   ★   ★

SCANS Note

Point out that human resources departments often can provide an official job description for each job within a company. In small companies without human resources departments, employers may be able to provide written job descriptions. Ask learners why it might be useful to have an official job description.

Teaching Note

Use this page to introduce the new language in the unit. Whenever possible, encourage peer teaching. Supply any language learners need.

Getting Started
Telling about job duties

TEAM WORK

What do these people do? Match the description with the picture. Can you think of other things these people might do at work?

a. She collects money from people who park.

b. She takes care of children.

c. He finds out what patients need.

d. He helps people with car trouble.

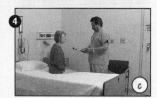

PARTNER WORK

Talk about the pictures. Student A asks questions. Student B answers.

A What does she do at work?

B She collects money from people who park.

 SURVEY

Work with a team. Ask team members about their jobs. What are their job duties? Make a list. Share your list with the class.

16   Unit 2

PREPARATION

To present or review **duties,** follow the procedure in Preparation on page 15.

PRESENTATION

1. Have learners read and discuss the Purpose Statement. For more information, see "Purpose Statement" on page viii.

2. Focus attention on the photographs. Encourage learners to say as much as they can about them. Write their ideas on the board and/or restate them in acceptable English.

3. Have teams read the Team Work instructions. Make sure each team knows what to do. Remind the teams that they are responsible for making sure that each member understands the new language. Then have teams

complete the activity. If learners need help, encourage them to consult other teams. Have team reporters share their answers with the class.

4. Have partners read the Partner Work instructions. Make sure partners know what to do. Then have partners complete the activity. Have learners switch partners and repeat the activity. Supply any language needed. Have one or two partners present their dialogs to the class.

5. Have teams read the Survey instructions. Make sure each learner knows what to do. Then have teams complete the activity. Have teams share their answers with the class. For more information, see "Survey" on page viii.

FOLLOW-UP

Job Descriptions: Ask partners to help each other write job descriptions of their current jobs or of jobs they would like to have. Have several learners read their descriptions to the class.

♦ Ask partners to examine the job descriptions they wrote and say how someone might acquire those skills. Which skills are best learned on the job? In school? Ask several pairs to share their ideas with the class.

WORKBOOK

Unit 2, Exercises 2A–2B

Talk About It — Explaining why your job is important

 PRACTICE THE DIALOG

A What do you do at the food mart, Steve?

B I'm a shift manager.

A What does a shift manager do?

B I take care of customer complaints, help customers find things, get change for the cashiers, and take deliveries. I like it when I can help customers find what they're looking for. That way, they keep coming back to the store.

A That sounds interesting.

B It is. My job's important because I know what's going on in the store during my shift. I make sure that the store runs smoothly.

 PARTNER WORK

Tell your partner why your job's important and how you feel when you do a good job. Use the dialog above and the Useful Language.

Useful Language

It's my job to . . .

I feel good when . . .

ASAP PROJECT

Work with a team to find four or five help wanted ads. For each ad, write the skills, the duties, and other people at the workplace who depend on the people with these jobs. Complete this project as you work through the unit.

Unit 2   17

ASAP PROJECT

Have learners read the instructions. Discuss the project and its purpose with learners. Make sure that everyone understands. Distribute "Help Wanted" sections of the newspaper to teams. Have each team select a leader, and have the team leaders or the whole class select an overall project leader. Throughout the rest of the unit, allow time for learners to work on the project. Have the teams agree on a deadline when the project will be finished. For more information, see "ASAP Project" on page vi.

PREPARATION

1. Display a picture of a house. Ask learners to name jobs involved in building houses, such as roofer and carpenter. Ask learners why each is important.

2. Use picture cards, explanation, pantomime, and role-play to present or review **complaints, cashiers, shift manager, deliveries,** and **runs smoothly.**

PRESENTATION

1. Have learners read and discuss the Purpose Statement. For more information, see "Purpose Statement" on page viii.

 2. Focus attention on the illustration. Encourage learners to say as much as they can about it. Write their ideas on the board and/or express them in acceptable English. Then present the dialog. See "Presenting a Dialog" on page ix.

3. Have partners read the Partner Work instructions. Focus attention on the Useful Language box. Help learners read the expressions. If necessary, model pronunciation. Then have learners complete the activity. Have learners switch partners and repeat the activity. Have one or two pairs present their dialogs to the class.

FOLLOW-UP

The Memory Game: Have the class work in teams. The first learner completes the sentence: "I feel good when _____," by filling in an accomplishment at work or school. The next learner repeats the statement ("Mario feels good when _____") and adds a similar statement. Have learners continue until everyone has participated. Ask several teams to repeat their lists for the class.

♦ Have teams write their statements. Check their work.

WORKBOOK

Unit 2, Exercises 3A–3B

Culture Note

Everyone makes mistakes. Discuss with learners why it is better to admit mistakes than to try to cover them up. Have volunteers provide examples from their workplace experiences that illustrate the point.

Personal Dictionary

Have learners add the words in their Personal Dictionary to their *Workforce Writing Dictionary*. For more information, see "Workforce Writing Dictionary" on page v.

Keep Talking Learning from experience

TEAM WORK

What went wrong? What did these people learn?

PARTNER WORK

What are the people thinking? Match the sentence with the picture above.

> a. Tomorrow I'll check the weather report before work.
> b. Next time I'll check the gas gauge sooner.
> c. Next time I'll set a timer.

PARTNER WORK

Tell your partner about a time you or someone you know solved a problem because of experience with that kind of problem.

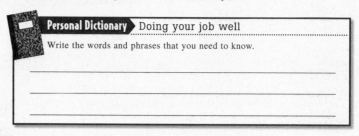

Personal Dictionary ▶ Doing your job well

Write the words and phrases that you need to know.

_____

_____

_____

18   Unit 2

PREPARATION

Use realia or picture cards to present or review **timer, gas gauge,** and **weather report.** Ask learners how these items have been helpful to them.

PRESENTATION

1. Have learners read the Purpose Statement. For more information, see "Purpose Statement" on page viii.

2. Focus attention on the illustrations. Encourage learners to say as much as they can about them. Write their ideas on the board and/or restate them in acceptable English.

3. Have teams read the Team Work instructions. Make sure everyone knows what to do. Model the activity if necessary. Then have teams complete the activity. Have team reporters share

their answers with the class.

4. Have partners read the Partner Work instructions. If necessary, model the activity. Allow learners time to complete the activity. Have pairs share their answers with the class.

5. Have partners read the Partner Work instructions. Make sure each partner knows what to do. If necessary, model the activity. Then have partners complete the activity. Ask partners to share their dialogs with the class.

6. Have learners read the Personal Dictionary instructions. Then use the Personal Dictionary procedures on page ix. Remind learners to continue to add words to their dictionaries throughout the unit.

FOLLOW-UP

Problem Solving: Write sentences such as the following on the board: *A carpenter runs out of nails. A seamstress buys cloth from two different dye lots.* Have teams describe what the workers will probably do differently next time. Have teams compare ideas.

♦ Have teams talk about things they learned from experience. Have volunteers share their ideas with the class.

WORKBOOK

Unit 2, Exercises 4A–4B

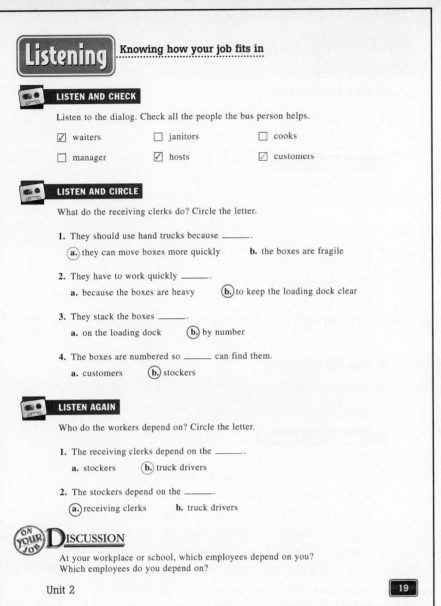

Listening — Knowing how your job fits in

LISTEN AND CHECK

Listen to the dialog. Check all the people the bus person helps.

- ☑ waiters
- ☐ janitors
- ☐ cooks
- ☐ manager
- ☑ hosts
- ☑ customers

LISTEN AND CIRCLE

What do the receiving clerks do? Circle the letter.

1. They should use hand trucks because _____.
   - **(a.)** they can move boxes more quickly
   - **b.** the boxes are fragile

2. They have to work quickly _____.
   - **a.** because the boxes are heavy
   - **(b.)** to keep the loading dock clear

3. They stack the boxes _____.
   - **a.** on the loading dock
   - **(b.)** by number

4. The boxes are numbered so _____ can find them.
   - **a.** customers
   - **(b.)** stockers

LISTEN AGAIN

Who do the workers depend on? Circle the letter.

1. The receiving clerks depend on the _____.
   - **a.** stockers
   - **(b.)** truck drivers

2. The stockers depend on the _____.
   - **(a.)** receiving clerks
   - **b.** truck drivers

DISCUSSION

At your workplace or school, which employees depend on you?
Which employees do you depend on?

Unit 2 — 19

Teaching Note

Point out to learners that their jobs help others both directly and indirectly. A customer service representative, for example, helps customers directly and helps other employees indirectly by maintaining customer satisfaction.

PREPARATION

Use a picture card of employees working at a restaurant to teach or review **bus person, bus the table, host,** and **waiter/waitress.** Use a picture card of a loading dock to clarify **hand truck, receiving clerk,** and **loading dock.** Discuss what happens at a loading dock.

PRESENTATION

1. Have learners read and discuss the Purpose Statement. For more information, see "Purpose Statement" on page viii.

 2. Have learners read the Listen and Check instructions and the list of people. Use peer teaching to clarify any unfamiliar vocabulary. Make sure that everyone understands the instructions. If

necessary, model the first item. Then play the tape or read the Listening Transcript aloud two or more times as learners complete the activity. Have learners check their work. For more information, see "Presenting a Listening Activity" on page ix.

 3. Have learners read the Listen and Circle instructions. Then follow the procedures in 2.

 4. Have learners read the Listen Again instructions. Then follow the procedures in 2.

5. Have learners read the Discussion Instructions. Make sure everyone knows what to do. Then have learners work in teams to discuss the questions. Have team reporters share their ideas with the class.

FOLLOW-UP

Important Job: Ask learners to list all the people they help on their jobs. Have several learners share their lists with the class.

♦ Ask partners to explain to each other how each person on their lists would be affected if they failed to do their jobs correctly. Have several partners summarize their conversations for the class.

WORKBOOK

Unit 2, Exercise 5A–5B

Describe your job duties

Explain why your job is important

★   ★   ★   ★   ★

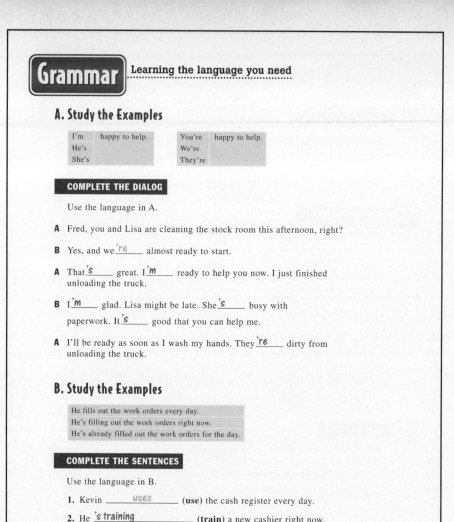

Grammar — Learning the language you need

A. Study the Examples

I'm	happy to help.
He's	
She's	

You're	happy to help.
We're	
They're	

COMPLETE THE DIALOG

Use the language in A.

A Fred, you and Lisa are cleaning the stock room this afternoon, right?

B Yes, and we _re_ almost ready to start.

A That _'s_ great. I _'m_ ready to help you now. I just finished unloading the truck.

B I _'m_ glad. Lisa might be late. She _'s_ busy with

paperwork. It _'s_ good that you can help me.

A I'll be ready as soon as I wash my hands. They _'re_ dirty from unloading the truck.

B. Study the Examples

He fills out the work orders every day.
He's filling out the work orders right now.
He's already filled out the work orders for the day.

COMPLETE THE SENTENCES

Use the language in B.

1. Kevin _____ uses _____ (**use**) the cash register every day.

2. He _'s training_ (**train**) a new cashier right now.

3. Selena _____ wants _____ (**want**) to learn how to use the cash register.

4. She _'s_ already _____ asked _____ (**ask**) Kevin to train her.

5. Kevin _____ likes _____ (**like**) to train employees.

20

Unit 2

PREPARATION

Review the language in the grammar boxes with learners before they open their books, if necessary.

PRESENTATION

1. Have learners read and discuss the Purpose Statement. For more information, see "Purpose Statement" on page viii. Use pantomime to teach or review **confused, shy,** and **upset.**

2. Have learners read the grammar boxes in A. Have learners use the language in the boxes to say as many sentences as possible. Tell learners that they can use the grammar boxes throughout the unit to review or check sentence structures.

3. Have learners read Complete the Dialog. If necessary, model the first item. Allow learners to complete the activity. Have partners check each other's work. Ask several partners to read the dialog aloud while the rest of the class checks their work.

4. Focus attention on the grammar box in B. Follow the procedures in 2.

5. Have learners read the instructions for Complete the Sentences. If necessary, model the first item. Then have learners complete the activity independently. Have a different learner read each sentence aloud as the rest of the class checks their answers.

C. Study the Examples

She feels	happy.
	sad.
	angry.
	disappointed.
	confused.
	hurt.
	shy.
	surprised.
	upset.
	good.

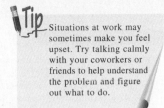

Tip Situations at work may sometimes make you feel upset. Try talking calmly with your coworkers or friends to help understand the problem and figure out what to do.

COMPLETE THE SENTENCES

Use the language in C.

1. Mona just got a raise. She probably _____*feels happy*_____.

2. Peter's boss told him to do one thing, and his coworker told him to do another. He probably _____*feels confused*_____.

3. Pablo and Ben got promotions. They probably _____*feel happy*_____.

4. Yolanda's company is closing. Yolanda probably _____*feels upset*_____.

PARTNER WORK

Ask your partner the questions. Write your partner's answer.

1. You have a new job. How do you feel?
   _____*I feel happy.*_____

2. You find out a friend got a job where you work. How do you feel?
   _____*Answers will vary.*_____

3. Your friend loses her job. How do you feel?
   _____

4. Your boss is unhappy with something you did at work. How do you feel?
   _____

5. You're very busy at work today. How do you feel?
   _____

Unit 2
21

---

6. Focus attention on the grammar box in C. Follow the procedures in 2.

7. Have learners read the instructions for Complete the Sentences. Then follow the procedures in 5.

8. Have learners read the Partner Work instructions. Make sure everyone knows what to do. If necessary, model the activity on the board. Then have partners complete the activity. Ask partners to share their answers with the class.

Tip Have learners read the Tip independently. Have learners discuss how the advice will help them. For more information, see "Presenting a Tip" on page ix.

FOLLOW-UP

Talking About Feelings: On separate slips of paper write sentences describing work situations that evoke uncomfortable feelings, for example, "A difficult customer upset you," or "A coworker made you angry." Place the slips in a basket and have each team take a slip. One team member should present the problem and the others should help that person calmly discuss and resolve the situation. Have teams exchange slips and repeat the activity. Have several teams present their dialogs to the class.

♦ Have learners discuss one of the uncomfortable situations with a partner. Then as a class, ask learners if they prefer talking about their feelings to one other person or to a small group. What are the advantages and disadvantages of each?

WORKBOOK

Unit 2, Exercises 6A–6C

BLACKLINE MASTERS

Blackline Master: Unit 2

Language Note

Help learners review the prepositions that commonly follow words expressing feelings. List phrases on the board, such as **sad about, angry at, disappointed by, hurt by,** *and* **surprised at** *or* **by.** *Ask learners to use the phrases in sentences.*

Language Note

Explain that job advertisements sometimes use different language to describe the same work. "Lawn care," for example, may also be described as "lawn maintenance." Underline examples in your local newspaper and pass the newspaper around the class. Help learners find additional examples.

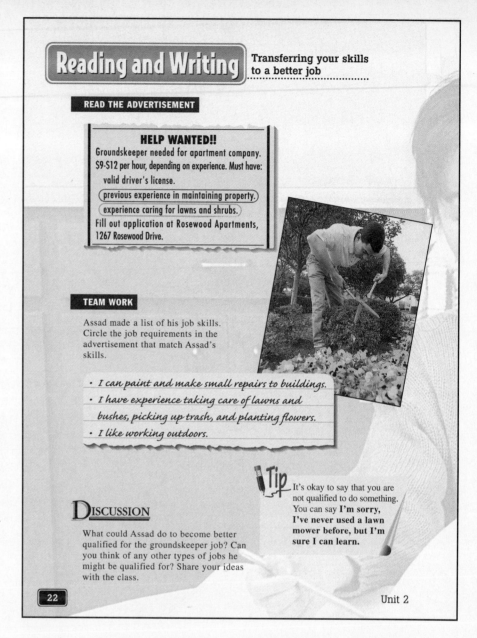

Reading and Writing Transferring your skills to a better job

READ THE ADVERTISEMENT

HELP WANTED!!
Groundskeeper needed for apartment company. $9-$12 per hour, depending on experience. Must have:
valid driver's license.
previous experience in maintaining property.
experience caring for lawns and shrubs.
Fill out application at Rosewood Apartments, 1267 Rosewood Drive.

TEAM WORK

Assad made a list of his job skills. Circle the job requirements in the advertisement that match Assad's skills.

• I can paint and make small repairs to buildings.
• I have experience taking care of lawns and bushes, picking up trash, and planting flowers.
• I like working outdoors.

DISCUSSION

What could Assad do to become better qualified for the groundskeeper job? Can you think of any other types of jobs he might be qualified for? Share your ideas with the class.

Tip It's okay to say that you are not qualified to do something. You can say **I'm sorry, I've never used a lawn mower before, but I'm sure I can learn.**

22

Unit 2

PREPARATION

1. Display and discuss help wanted ads. Give teams a few ads each and ask them to circle the skills in the ads.

2. Use realia, pictures, and/or explanation to present or review **groundskeeper, valid driver's license, property, lawn,** and **shrubs.**

PRESENTATION

1. Have learners read and discuss the Purpose Statement. For more information, see "Purpose Statement" on page viii.

2. Have learners preview the job ad before they read. See "Prereading" on page x. Encourage learners to say everything they can about the ad and the photograph. Write their ideas on the board and/or restate them in acceptable English. Then have them read the ad independently.

3. Have teams read the Team Work instructions. Make sure each team knows what to do. Then have teams complete the activity. If learners need help, encourage them to consult other teams. Have team reporters share their answers with the class.

4. Have learners read the Discussion instructions. Make sure everyone knows what to do. Then have learners work in teams to answer the questions. Have team reporters share their teams' ideas with the class. Have teams compare ideas.

Tip Have learners read the Tip independently. Have learners discuss how the advice will help them. For more information, see "Presenting a Tip" on page ix.

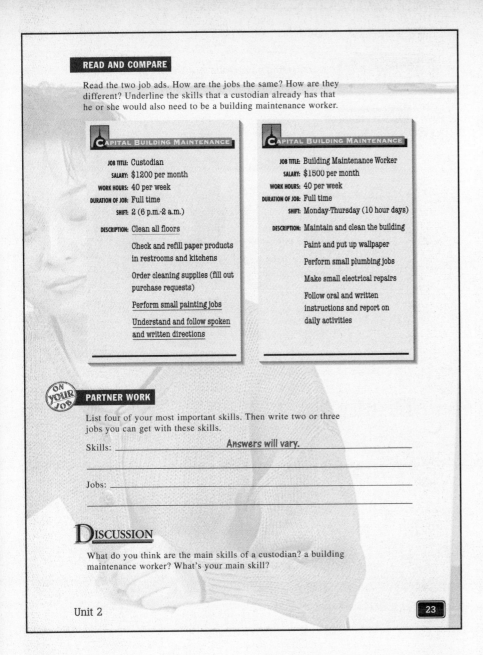

READ AND COMPARE

Read the two job ads. How are the jobs the same? How are they different? Underline the skills that a custodian already has that he or she would also need to be a building maintenance worker.

CAPITAL BUILDING MAINTENANCE

JOB TITLE: Custodian
SALARY: $1200 per month
WORK HOURS: 40 per week
DURATION OF JOB: Full time
SHIFT: 2 (6 p.m.-2 a.m.)

DESCRIPTION: Clean all floors

Check and refill paper products in restrooms and kitchens

Order cleaning supplies (fill out purchase requests)

Perform small painting jobs

Understand and follow spoken and written directions

CAPITAL BUILDING MAINTENANCE

JOB TITLE: Building Maintenance Worker
SALARY: $1500 per month
WORK HOURS: 40 per week
DURATION OF JOB: Full time
SHIFT: Monday-Thursday (10 hour days)

DESCRIPTION: Maintain and clean the building

Paint and put up wallpaper

Perform small plumbing jobs

Make small electrical repairs

Follow oral and written instructions and report on daily activities

PARTNER WORK

List four of your most important skills. Then write two or three jobs you can get with these skills.

Skills: _____ Answers will vary. _____

_____

Jobs: _____

_____

DISCUSSION

What do you think are the main skills of a custodian? a building maintenance worker? What's your main skill?

Unit 2
23

5. Have learners preview the job postings before they read. See "Prereading" on page x. Encourage learners to say as much as they can about the postings. Write learners' ideas on the board and/or restate them in acceptable English.

6. Have learners read the Read and Compare instructions. Make sure that everyone understands the instructions. If necessary, model the activity. Then have learners complete the activity. Have one or two learners read their answers while the rest of the class checks their work.

7. Have partners read the Partner Work instructions. Model the activity if necessary by suggesting skills and jobs. Then have partners complete the activity. Have learners switch partners and repeat the activity. Have one or two pairs present their answers to the class.

8. Have learners read the Discussion instructions. Model the activity if necessary by suggesting your main skills. Then have learners complete the activity. Have them discuss their answers with team members. Have team reporters summarize the discussions for the class. Ask teams to compare ideas.

FOLLOW-UP

The Match Game: Cut out pairs of help wanted ads for entry-level and advanced jobs in the same category, such as gardener and landscape designer or file clerk and office manager. Prepare enough pairs of ads that there is one ad for each learner. Mount the ads on cards. Give one card to each student, and have each learner find the learner with the related job.

♦ Ask teams to discuss ways the entry-level employees could gain skills to obtain the advanced jobs. Have team reporters share their ideas with the class.

WORKBOOK

Unit 2, Exercises 7A–7B

Extension ········ Transferring your skills to a better job

READ THE STORY

Changing Jobs

Lyle worked as a carpenter when he lived in Texas. When he moved to Illinois, he applied for a job as a clerk in a hardware store. He did very well in his interview, and the people at the hardware store hired him. Lyle liked his work, and his new job made him feel secure. Because of his past experience as a carpenter he was a good hardware clerk.

Then Lyle decided to study bookkeeping at night. He went to school for two years. Then the hardware store had an opening for a bookkeeper. Lyle applied for the job. Because of his past job experience, Lyle knew the hardware store's products very well. He also understood bookkeeping. Everyone thought Lyle was a good choice for store bookkeeper.

DISCUSSION

How did Lyle use his skills and develop new ones? How can you get the skills you need to move up?

  **CultureNotes**

You find out that your company has an opening for a better job. You think you're qualified for the job. Who do you talk to? Why? What do you say?

24　　　　　　　　　　　　　　　　　　　　　　　　Unit 2

Culture Note

Explain that the average worker will change jobs a number of times during his or her working life. Discuss reasons for this phenomenon, such as personal ambition, plant closings, changes in product and service needs in a community, and worker mobility. Ask volunteers to explain reasons they've changed jobs.

PREPARATION

Use realia or pictures to teach or review **carpenter, hardware,** and **bookkeeper.**

PRESENTATION

1. Have learners read and discuss the Purpose Statement. For more information, see "Purpose Statement" on page viii.

2. Have learners preview the information in the article. Encourage them to say everything they can about the article. Write their ideas on the board and/or restate them in acceptable English. Then have learners read the article independently. For more information, see "Prereading" on page x.

3. Have learners read the Discussion instructions. Model the activity if

necessary by talking about the training you received to become qualified to teach the class. Have learners complete the activity independently and then discuss their ideas in teams. Have team reporters share their ideas with the class.

4. Have learners read Culture Notes and talk over their responses in teams. Have team reporters share ideas with the class. Ask the teams to compare each other's ideas. For more information, see "Culture Notes" on page vii.

FOLLOW-UP

Transferring Skills: Ask each learner to create a two column chart. In the first column, learners should list skills they use at their workplace; in the second

column, they should tell where they learned the skill. Then have learners work in pairs to rearrange the charts so each learner's skills are listed in order from the first skill they learned to the most recent. Post the charts.

◆ Tape a blank sheet of paper next to each chart. Ask pairs to circulate from chart to chart and think of other jobs the learner could do with his or her skills. They should write their ideas on the blank paper. Then return the charts to the original learners. Have one or two learners read the suggestions they received to the class.

WORKBOOK

Unit 2, Exercise 8

 **Performance Check** How well can you use the skills in this unit?
....

Complete the activities. Go over your work with a partner or your teacher.
Then complete the Performance Review on page 26.

SKILL 1 | DESCRIBE YOUR JOB DUTIES

Your partner or your teacher is interested in applying for a job
like yours. Tell him or her about your job duties.

SKILL 2 | EXPLAIN WHY YOUR JOB IS IMPORTANT

Tell your partner or your teacher why your job's important.
Explain how you work with other people at your workplace
or school.

SKILL 3 | TRANSFER YOUR SKILLS TO A BETTER JOB

Underline the skills that a food prep worker already has that he
or she would also need to be a cook.

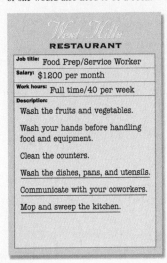

West Hills
RESTAURANT

Job title: Food Prep/Service Worker
Salary: $1200 per month
Work hours: Full time/40 per week
Description:

Wash the fruits and vegetables.

Wash your hands before handling
food and equipment.

Clean the counters.

Wash the dishes, pans, and utensils.

Communicate with your coworkers.

Mop and sweep the kitchen.

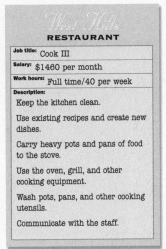

West Hills
RESTAURANT

Job title: Cook III
Salary: $1460 per month
Work hours: Full time/40 per week
Description:

Keep the kitchen clean.

Use existing recipes and create new
dishes.

Carry heavy pots and pans of food
to the stove.

Use the oven, grill, and other
cooking equipment.

Wash pots, pans, and other cooking
utensils.

Communicate with the staff.

Unit 2

25

PRESENTATION

Use any of the procedures in
"Evaluation," page x, with pages 25 and
26. Record individuals' results on the
Unit 2 Individual Competency Chart.
Record the class's results on the Class
Cumulative Competency Chart.

Tell your partner or teacher about a time when you or someone you know solved a problem because of experience with that kind of problem.

Performance Review

I can...

☐ 1. describe my job duties.

☐ 2. explain why my job is important.

☐ 3. transfer my skills to a better job.

☐ 4. learn from experience.

DISCUSSION

Work with a team. How will the skills help you? Make a list. Share the list with your class.

Unit 2

PRESENTATION

Follow the instructions on page 25.

INFORMAL WORKPLACE-SPECIFIC ASSESSMENT

Ask learners to describe a job they would like to have someday. Ask them which skills they already have for this job and which they still need to learn. Discuss ideas for acquiring the new skills.

WORKBOOK

Unit 2, Exercise 9

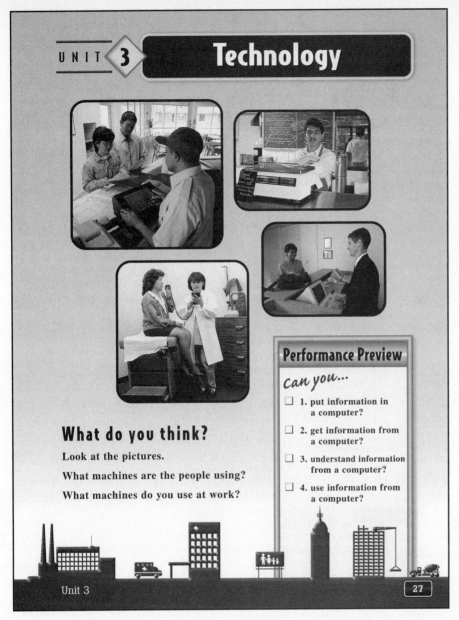

UNIT 3 — Technology

What do you think?

Look at the pictures.

What machines are the people using?

What machines do you use at work?

Performance Preview

can you...

☐ 1. put information in a computer?

☐ 2. get information from a computer?

☐ 3. understand information from a computer?

☐ 4. use information from a computer?

Unit 3 Overview
—SCANS Competencies—

★ Apply technology to specific tasks

★ Acquire and evaluate information

★ Select equipment and tools

★ Understand technological systems

★ Use computers to process information

Workforce Skills

• Put information in a computer

• Get information from a computer

• Understand information from a computer

• Use information from a computer

Materials

• Picture cards of computers and of machines with computers, such as a scale, cash register, thermometer, and handheld scanner; products displaying bar codes; cash register receipts; various computer printouts; two dozen or more pens and pencils of different sorts; at-home shopping catalog for popcorn products; picture cards of an auto repair shop and a veterinarian; a debit card

Unit Warm-Up

To get the learners thinking about the unit topic (using computers to process information), show learners picture cards of computers and machines with computers. Have learners name the machines and/or describe their use.

★   ★   ★   ★   ★

WORKFORCE SKILLS (page 27)

Put information in a computer

Get information from a computer

★   ★   ★   ★   ★

PREPARATION

Show learners a computer or a picture of a computer. Help learners identify the various components, such as the keyboard, monitor, screen, and mouse.

PRESENTATION

1. Focus attention on the photographs. Ask learners to speculate what the unit might be about. Write their ideas on the board and/or restate them in acceptable English.

2. Have learners talk about the photographs. Ask them to point out the computer in each, and explain how information is put into and retrieved from each one.

3. Help learners read the questions. Discuss the questions with the class.

4. You may want to use the Performance Preview to provide learners with an overview of the skills in the unit. Have learners read the list of skills and discuss what they will learn.

FOLLOW-UP

Computers at Work: Give each of four teams a picture card of a computer or of a machine that incorporates a computer. Write these questions on the board:

Where is this machine used?

What does it do?

Who uses it?

Have teams discuss the questions. Then put all the pictures on the chalk rail in random order. As team reporters answer the questions aloud, ask other teams to indicate the appropriate picture.

♦ Return pictures to their original teams. Ask learners to think of the people or machines that used to perform the same tasks in the day before computers. Ask team leaders to share the teams' ideas with the class.

WORKBOOK

Unit 3, Exercises 1A–1C

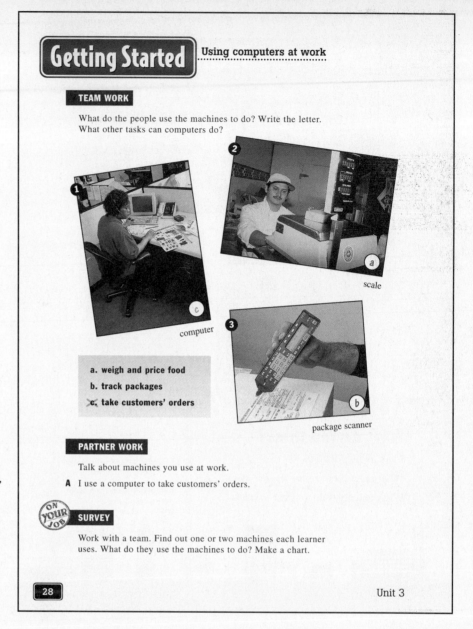

SCANS Note

Discuss how computers affect the amount of time people spend on different tasks, accuracy in the workplace, and customer service. Encourage learners to use examples from their own workplaces.

Teaching Note

Use this page to introduce the new language in the unit. Whenever possible, encourage peer teaching. Supply any language learners need.

PREPARATION

Share with learners how you use computers or information from computers, such as preparing hand-outs. Encourage learners' questions about how computers help you.

PRESENTATION

1. Have learners read and discuss the Purpose Statement. For more information, see "Purpose Statement" on page viii.

2. Focus attention on the photographs. Encourage learners to say as much as they can about them. Write their ideas on the board and/or restate them in acceptable English. Then have teams read the Team Work instructions. Make sure each team knows what to do. If necessary, model the first item. Remind

the teams that they are responsible for making sure that each member understands the new language. Then have teams complete the activity. Have team reporters share their answers with the class.

3. Have partners read the Partner Work instructions. Make sure partners know what to do. Then have partners complete the activity. Have learners switch partners and repeat the activity. Have one or two pairs present their dialogs to the class.

4. Have teams read the Survey instructions. Make sure each learner knows what to do. Then have teams complete the activity. Have teams share their charts with the class. See "Survey," page viii.

FOLLOW-UP

Bar Graph: Using the charts from the Survey, help the class tally the total number of learners who use each machine. Then help them create a bar graph showing the frequency of use of the top six machines. The horizontal axis should show the machines; the vertical axis, the number of learners.

◆ Assign one of the six machines to each team. Have teams prepare and give presentations that explain how the machine benefits a company and its employees.

WORKBOOK

Unit 3, Exercises 2A–2B

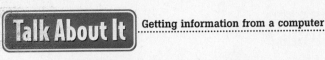

Getting information from a computer

PRACTICE THE DIALOG

A This bar code is on all our products. The bar code tells the computer what product has been purchased.

B How does it work?

A You pass the product over this glass plate. The computer reads the bar code.

B Then the computer knows all about the item?

A Yes, the computer knows the name and price of the product and prints them on the receipt.

PARTNER WORK

Talk about the kinds of information you can get from a computer at your workplace or school. Use the dialog and the Useful Language above.

ASAP PROJECT

Work with a team to find out about computer training where you live. Look for information in a local newspaper and phone book. Also check libraries, schools, and community colleges. Make a list of training that's available. Include the cost, location, and any requirements for taking the training. Complete this project as you work through the unit.

Unit 3

29

Useful Language

The computer can tell us . . .

    the amount of tax.

    the total bill.

    the number of items.

    the date and time.

    the items in the warehouse.

    each customer's order.

ASAP PROJECT

Have learners read the instructions. Discuss the project and its purpose with learners. Make sure that everyone understands. If possible, bring in catalogs from local technical schools or community colleges. Help learners assign themselves to teams based upon their knowledge, skills, interests, or other individual strengths. Have each team select a leader, and have the team leaders or the whole class select an overall project leader. Throughout the rest of the unit, allow time for learners to work on the project. Have the teams agree on a deadline when the project will be finished. For more information, see "ASAP Project" on page vi.

PREPARATION

1. Point out and identify the bar codes on various products. Help learners name the types of information bar codes can access, such as product names and prices.

2. Pass receipts around the class. Ask learners how information about products ends up on receipts.

PRESENTATION

1. Have learners read and discuss the Purpose Statement. For more information, see "Purpose Statement" on page viii.

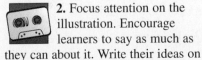 **2.** Focus attention on the illustration. Encourage learners to say as much as they can about it. Write their ideas on the board and/or restate them in acceptable English. Then present the dialog. See "Presenting a Dialog" on page ix.

3. Have partners read the Partner Work instructions. Focus attention on the Useful Language box. Help learners read the expressions. If necessary, model pronunciation. Then have learners complete the activity. Have learners switch partners and repeat the activity. Have one or two pairs present their dialogs to the class.

FOLLOW-UP

Dialogs: Give each pair a store receipt. Have one partner role-play a customer who requests an explanation of the receipt. Have the other partner role-play the cashier who provides the explanation. Ask several pairs to present their dialogs to the class.

♦ Have partners write their dialogs.

WORKBOOK

Unit 3, Exercise 3

★　　★　　★　　★　　★

Culture Note

Discuss with learners that many public libraries make computers available to the public at no cost to the user. Explain that, often, library personnel are available to help people use the computers. Discuss reasons learners might make use of such services, such as accessing tax forms or telephone directories in other cities, or looking at job listings.

Personal Dictionary

Have learners add the words in their Personal Dictionary to their *Workforce Writing Dictionary.* For more information, see "Workforce Writing Dictionary" on page v.

 **Keep Talking** .... Understanding information from a computer

TEAM WORK

Look at the printout. What information did the computer provide? How can it be used?

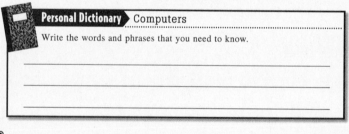

the box store		INVENTORY		
TYPE OF BOX	SIZE	LAST MONTH'S INVENTORY	CURRENT INVENTORY	BOXES SOLD LAST MONTH
Small	2 feet x 2 feet	500	130	370
Medium	3 feet x 3 feet	600	252	348
Large	4 feet x 3.5 feet	450	90	360

 PRACTICE THE DIALOG

A How many small boxes did we sell last month?

B The last column lists the number of boxes we sold. The printout says we sold 370 small boxes.

PARTNER WORK

Take turns asking and answering questions about the printout. Follow the dialog above.

 DISCUSSION

What kinds of computer printouts have you seen at your workplace or school? What information do they provide?

Personal Dictionary ▷ Computers

Write the words and phrases that you need to know.

_____

_____

_____

30   Unit 3

PREPARATION

1. Display various computer printouts. Ask learners to refer to them as they discuss different functions computers can perform, such as mathematical computations and information retrieval.

2. Encourage learners who use inventory printouts at work to talk about how they use them.

PRESENTATION

1. Have learners read the Purpose Statement. For more information, see "Purpose Statement" on page viii.

2. Focus attention on the inventory printout. Discuss with learners the kind of information it gives. Write learners' ideas on the board and/or restate them in acceptable English.

3. Have teams read the Team Work instructions. Make sure each team knows what to do. Then have teams answer the questions. Have team reporters share their answers with the class. Then present the dialog. See "Presenting a Dialog" on page ix.

4. Have partners read the Partner Work instructions and complete the activity. Have learners change partners and repeat. Have partners share their dialogs with the class.

 5. Have learners read the Discussion instructions. Make sure everyone knows what to do. Then have learners work in teams to discuss computer printouts they've seen. Have team reporters share their teams' ideas with the class.

6. Have learners read the Personal Dictionary instructions. Then use the Personal Dictionary procedures on page ix. Remind learners to add words to their dictionaries throughout the unit.

FOLLOW-UP

Create an Inventory: Display two dozen or more pencils and pens of various sorts. Help learners sort the items and create an inventory to show the number of items in stock in each category.

♦ Remove some of the pens and pencils. Explain that these items were sold. Ask learners to add columns to their inventories to show the number of items sold and on hand.

WORKBOOK

Unit 3, Exercise 4

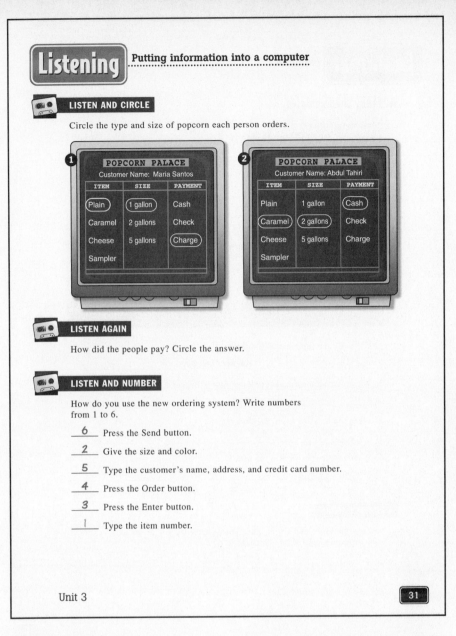

Listening · Putting information into a computer

LISTEN AND CIRCLE

Circle the type and size of popcorn each person orders.

1 POPCORN PALACE
Customer Name: Maria Santos

ITEM	SIZE	PAYMENT
(Plain)	(1 gallon)	Cash
Caramel	2 gallons	Check
Cheese	5 gallons	(Charge)
Sampler		

2 POPCORN PALACE
Customer Name: Abdul Tahiri

ITEM	SIZE	PAYMENT
Plain	1 gallon	(Cash)
(Caramel)	(2 gallons)	Check
Cheese	5 gallons	Charge
Sampler		

LISTEN AGAIN

How did the people pay? Circle the answer.

LISTEN AND NUMBER

How do you use the new ordering system? Write numbers from 1 to 6.

__6__ Press the Send button.

__2__ Give the size and color.

__5__ Type the customer's name, address, and credit card number.

__4__ Press the Order button.

__3__ Press the Enter button.

__1__ Type the item number.

Unit 3

31

SCANS Note

Suggest that learners keep a personal employment record that includes their employers' names and addresses, their supervisors' names, and their dates of employment. Encourage learners who have access to personal computers to prepare the record on the computer. Ask how this will help when learners need to update the record.

PREPARATION

Use picture cards, realia, or product catalogs to present or review **popcorn, plain, caramel, cheese, sampler,** and **gallon.**

PRESENTATION

1. Have learners read and discuss the Purpose Statement. For more information, see "Purpose Statement" on page viii.

2. Focus attention on the computer screens. Have learners discuss the type of information on the screens and its purpose.

 3. Have learners read the Listen and Circle instructions. Make sure that everyone understands what to do. If necessary, model the first item. Then play the tape or read the Listening Transcript aloud two or more times as learners complete the activity. Have learners check their work. For more information, see "Presenting a Listening Activity" on page ix.

 4. Have learners read the Listen Again instructions. Then follow the procedures in 3.

 5. Have learners read the Listen and Number instructions. Then follow the procedures in 3.

FOLLOW-UP

Order Screen: Have teams design an order screen for a cash register in an ice cream shop. On the board, write: **vanilla, chocolate, strawberry, chocolate chip, small, medium, large, cone, cup, cash, check,** and **charge.**

Have teams organize the information in four categories so an employee can enter customers' orders easily. Learners should label the categories. Have teams compare screens.

♦ Have team members take turns as the cashier in the ice cream shop who takes customers' orders. Other team members act as customers for each cashier. As a class, discuss how the order screen helps the cashier know what questions to ask the customer.

WORKBOOK

Unit 3, Exercise 5

Put information in a computer

Get information from a computer

★ ★ ★ ★ ★

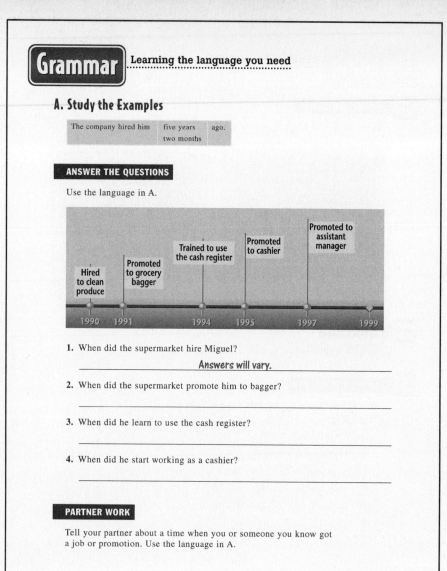

Grammar
Learning the language you need

A. Study the Examples

| The company hired him | five years two months | ago. |

ANSWER THE QUESTIONS

Use the language in A.

Hired to clean produce — 1990
Promoted to grocery bagger — 1991
Trained to use the cash register — 1994
Promoted to cashier — 1995
Promoted to assistant manager — 1997
1999

1. When did the supermarket hire Miguel?

_____ Answers will vary. _____

2. When did the supermarket promote him to bagger?

_____

3. When did he learn to use the cash register?

_____

4. When did he start working as a cashier?

_____

PARTNER WORK

Tell your partner about a time when you or someone you know got a job or promotion. Use the language in A.

`32`

Unit 3

PREPARATION

Review the language in the grammar boxes with learners before they open their books, if necessary. Role-play a company manager talking about hiring and promoting employees to teach or review **hire** and **promote**.

PRESENTATION

1. Have learners read and discuss the Purpose Statement. For more information, see "Purpose Statement" on page viii.

2. Have learners read the grammar box in A. Have learners use the language in the box to say as many sentences as possible. Tell learners that they can use the grammar boxes throughout the unit to review or check sentence structures.

3. Focus attention on Answer the

Questions. Have learners read the questions. If necessary, model the first item. Then have learners complete the activity independently. Have a different learner read each question and answer aloud as the rest of the class checks their answers.

4. Have learners read the Partner Work instructions. Make sure everyone knows what to do. Then have partners complete the activity. Have learners change partners and repeat. Ask several partners to share their dialogs with the class.

B. Study the Examples

How long has she worked for this company?

| She's worked for this company since | 1970. June. | She's worked for this company for | five years. one week. |

COMPLETE THE SENTENCES

Give the correct form of the verb. Circle the word *for* or *since*.

1. Hong _'s worked_____ (**work**) at this company (for) / since ten years.

2. I _'ve been_____ (**be**) a data entry clerk (for) / since two months.

3. My sister _'s used_____ (**use**) a calculator for / (since) 1995.

4. The plumbers _____have used_____ (**use**) computer reports (for) / since a month.

5. Our supplier _____has used_____ (**use**) bar codes for / (since) May.

6. We _'ve kept_____ (**keep**) customer records on the computer for / (since) 1994.

7. We _'ve had_____ (**have**) computer problems for / (since) 9:00 this morning.

TEAM WORK

Tell about Nora's work history. Use the language in B.

1987 · Began work
1990 · Learned how to use a computer
1993 · Became a computer specialist
1998 · Became a customer service manager
2000

1. How long has Nora worked for the company?
2. How long has she known how to use a computer?
3. How long did she work as a computer specialist?
4. How long has she been a customer service manager?

Unit 3   33

---

5. Focus attention on the grammar boxes in B. Follow the procedures in 2.

6. Have learners read the instructions for Complete the Sentences. If necessary, model the first item on the board. Then have learners complete the activity independently. Have a different learner read each sentence aloud as the rest of the class checks their answers.

7. Have teams read the Team Work instructions. Make sure each team knows what to do. If necessary, model the first item. Then have teams complete the activity. If learners need help, encourage them to consult other teams. Have team reporters share their answers with the class.

FOLLOW-UP

History: Distribute several index cards to each learner. Ask learners to write one sentence on each card that describes how long they worked at each of their jobs or attended a school. For example, learners should write: *I worked at Joy Greeting Cards for ten months* or *I have attended Clark Community College since January.* Have pairs exchange cards. Ask learners to use the cards to present information about their partners to the class.

♦ Have learners arrange their cards in order and create timelines based on the information. Have them share their timelines with the class.

WORKBOOK

Unit 3, Exercises 6A–6E

BLACKLINE MASTERS

Blackline Master: Unit 3

★ ★ ★ ★ ★

Language Note

*Discuss that computer technology has introduced new words to the language and new meanings for existing words. Give examples in each category. For instance, new words include **modem**, **software**, and **CD-ROM**; words with new meanings include **mouse** and **hardware**. Ask learners for more examples.*

Reading and Writing — Using information from a computer

READ THE ARTICLE

Computers at Work

These days, almost every business uses computers. With computers, employees can organize and find information quickly. There are many ways to use a computer to help a business.

An auto repair shop might have information on the computer about every car that has been worked on, what was done to the car, how much was charged, and when the car will need maintenance. The shop's manager can make a list of customers whose cars need an oil change.

A computer in a veterinarian's office might have information about customers' pets. The vet's assistant can look up the names of owners whose pets need shots and contact the owners.

Hotel computers have information about which rooms have guests in them and about check-out dates. The hotel housekeeping staff can easily find out which rooms need cleaning.

A grocery store computer has information about how much things cost. The groceries are marked with bar codes. The price of the groceries might change, but the bar code doesn't change. With bar codes and computers to read them, the clerks don't have to mark the groceries every time the manager changes prices. The manager goes to the computer and changes the price that goes with that bar code.

Computers help people do their jobs. They help businesses run better. As customers and as workers, all of us are familiar with this new, helpful technology.

WRITE THE LETTER

| a. when pets need their shots | b. bar code |
| c. need to have an oil change | d. which rooms need cleaning |

1. A mechanic might make a list of customers whose cars ___c___.

2. A vet might store information about ___a___.

3. The hotel's computer lets the housekeepers know ___d___.

4. A supermarket manager can change prices of items on the computer, and the computer will use the ___b___ to look up the new price.

 PARTNER WORK

Think of a way that information from a computer can help at your workplace or school. Tell your partner.

34   Unit 3

PREPARATION

Use explanation, picture cards, or pantomime to present or review **auto repair shop, maintenance, oil change,** and **veterinarian.**

PRESENTATION

1. Have learners read and discuss the Purpose Statement. For more information, see "Purpose Statement" on page viii.

2. Have learners preview the article before they read. See "Prereading" on page x. Encourage learners to say everything they can about the article. Write their ideas on the board and/or restate them in acceptable English. Then have them read the article independently.

3. Have learners read the lettered items and the sentences in Write the Letter. Make sure everyone knows what to do. Model the first item on the board, if necessary. Then have learners complete the activity independently. Have learners review each other's work as partners. Ask several partners to share their answers with the class while the rest of the class checks their work.

4. Have learners read the Partner Work instructions. Make sure everyone knows what to do. Then have partners complete the activity. Have learners change partners and repeat. Ask one or two partners to share their dialogs with the class.

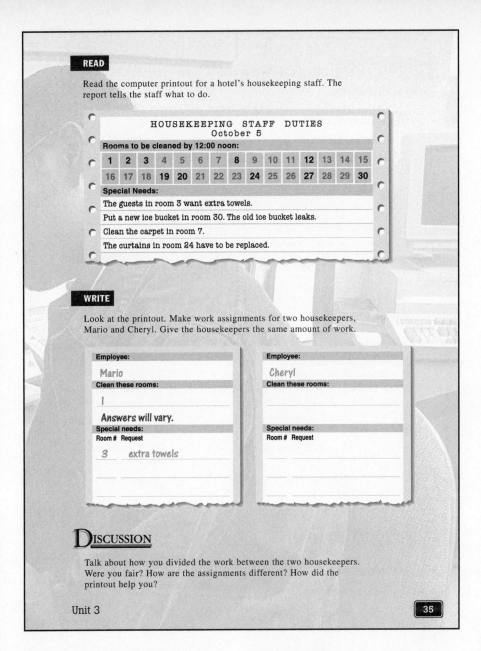

READ

Read the computer printout for a hotel's housekeeping staff. The report tells the staff what to do.

HOUSEKEEPING STAFF DUTIES
October 5

Rooms to be cleaned by 12:00 noon:

| 1 | 2 | 3 | 4 | 5 | 6 | 7 | 8 | 9 | 10 | 11 | 12 | 13 | 14 | 15 |
| 16 | 17 | 18 | 19 | 20 | 21 | 22 | 23 | 24 | 25 | 26 | 27 | 28 | 29 | 30 |

Special Needs:

The guests in room 3 want extra towels.

Put a new ice bucket in room 30. The old ice bucket leaks.

Clean the carpet in room 7.

The curtains in room 24 have to be replaced.

WRITE

Look at the printout. Make work assignments for two housekeepers, Mario and Cheryl. Give the housekeepers the same amount of work.

Employee:
Mario
Clean these rooms:
1
Answers will vary.
Special needs:
Room #   Request
3   extra towels

Employee:
Cheryl
Clean these rooms:

Special needs:
Room #   Request

DISCUSSION

Talk about how you divided the work between the two housekeepers. Were you fair? How are the assignments different? How did the printout help you?

Unit 3

35

---

5. Have learners preview the computer printout before they read. Follow the procedures in 2.

6. Have learners read the instructions for Write. Then focus attention on the housekeeping assignment forms. Discuss where learners write information. Remind them that the workers' assignments should be equal. Model the activity on the board, if necessary. Then have partners complete the activity independently.

7. Have learners read the Discussion instructions. Model the activity if necessary by comparing the differences in several learners' completed forms. Then have learners complete the activity in teams of three or four. Have team reporters summarize their teams' discussions for the class.

FOLLOW-UP

Computers in Business: Write the words "auto repair shop," "veterinarian's office," "hotel," and "grocery store" on slips of paper. Divide the class into four teams and have each team pick a slip. Ask teams to discuss ways the business could use a computer. What information could be on the computers? Who would use the computers? What would they use them for? Have team reporters summarize their discussions for the class.

♦ Have partners choose one of the businesses. Ask them to create dialogs in which an employee is using a computer to help a customer. Have several pairs present their dialogs to the class.

WORKBOOK

Unit 3, Exercises 7A–7B

Extension Using a debit machine

READ THE ARTICLE

HOW DO DEBIT CARDS WORK?

People use debit cards to get cash and to buy things. A debit card has a black magnetic strip on it. The strip contains computer information such as the customer's name, the bank's name, and the account number.

A debit machine is a computer that can read the magnetic strip. The debit machine uses this information to talk to the computer at the customer's bank. This allows a customer to use money in the account to get cash or to buy something. These computers do not let customers spend more than the money in their account.

To use a debit card, customers put it in the debit machine and follow the instructions. The machine will ask for a password. The password is a secret number that only the customer knows. This protects the customer's money if the card is stolen because no one can use the card without the password.

ANSWER THE QUESTIONS

Match each question in the left-hand column with the answer in the right-hand column. Write the letter of the answer on the line provided.

_b_ 1. What does the magnetic strip contain?

_a_ 2. Why is there a secret code?

_d_ 3. What can read the magnetic strip?

_c_ 4. Why do people use a debit card?

a. to protect the customer's money

b. the bank's name and the customer's account number

c. to buy things and get cash

d. a debit machine

 Culture Notes

When a workplace gets a new machine, people sometimes feel a little nervous about using it. Why do you think these people feel nervous? How do you feel about using a new machine at your workplace?

36   Unit 3

SCANS Note

Explain that some companies have employees whose job is to help other employees use computers. Ask learners who helps employees with computers at their workplace.

PREPARATION

1. Show learners a debit card. Point out the black magnetic strip. Discuss information that is encoded in the strip. Have volunteers describe how they use a debit card and/or tell learners how you use one.

2. To present or review **password,** tell learners that to protect people's bank accounts, most debit cards have a secret code customers type when they use their cards.

PRESENTATION

1. Have learners read and discuss the Purpose Statement. For more information, see "Purpose Statement" on page viii.

2. Have learners preview the information in the article. See

"Prereading" on page x. Encourage learners to say everything they can about the article. Write their ideas on the board and/or restate them in acceptable English. Then have them read the article independently.

3. Have learners read the instructions for Answer the Questions. Model the activity if necessary. Then have learners complete the activity independently. Have learners read their answers aloud while the class checks their responses.

 4. Have learners read Culture Notes and talk over their responses in teams. Have team reporters share their ideas with the class. Ask teams to compare ideas. For more information, see "Culture Notes" on page vii.

FOLLOW-UP

Debit Card and Credit Cards: Have teams discuss debit cards and credit cards. How are they the same? How are they different? How do people get each kind of card? What should people do if the cards are lost or stolen? Have team reporters share ideas with the class.

♦ Poll the class. How many learners work at places where customers can use debit cards to purchase products or services. Credit cards? Both? Write the numbers on the board. Ask learners why they think their workplaces do or do not accept these cards.

WORKBOOK

Unit 3, Exercise 8

Performance Check How well can you use the skills in this unit?

Complete the activities. Go over your work with a partner or your teacher. Then complete the Performance Review on page 38.

SKILL 1 ▌ **PUT INFORMATION IN A COMPUTER**

Listen to the customer place his order. Circle the information on the computer screen.

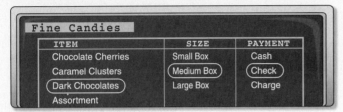

ITEM	SIZE	PAYMENT
Chocolate Cherries	Small Box	Cash
Caramel Clusters	(Medium Box)	(Check)
(Dark Chocolates)	Large Box	Charge
Assortment		

Fine Candies

SKILL 2 ▌ **GET INFORMATION FROM A COMPUTER**

What kinds of information can you get from a computer at your workplace or school? Tell a partner or your teacher.

SKILL 3 ▌ **UNDERSTAND INFORMATION FROM A COMPUTER**

Look at the printout. How many small pizza boxes did the Pizza Pavillion use in August? Tell your partner or your teacher.

PIZZA PAVILLION   Pizza Box Inventory

Type of Box	Size	August Inventory	September Inventory	Boxes Used
Small	12 inches x 12 inches x 2 inches	500	275	225
Medium	14 inches x 14 inches x 2 inches	500	110	390
Large	16 inches x 16 inches x 2 inches	600	208	392

Unit 3   37

PRESENTATION

Use any of the procedures in "Evaluation," page x, with pages 37 and 38. Record individuals' results on the Unit 3 Individual Competency Chart. Record the class's results on the Class Cumulative Competency Chart.

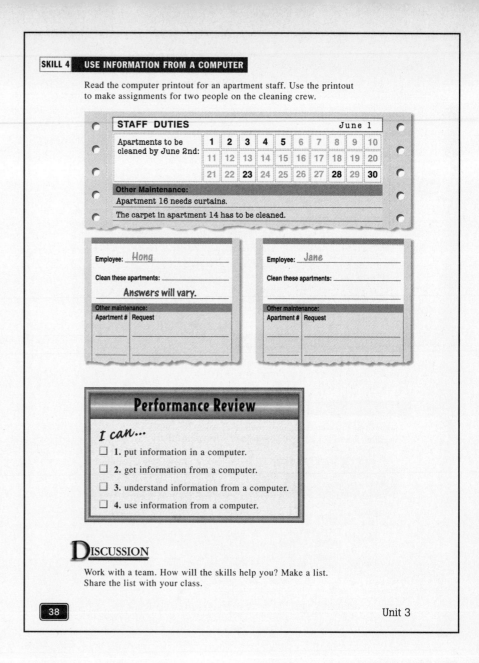

SKILL 4   **USE INFORMATION FROM A COMPUTER**

Read the computer printout for an apartment staff. Use the printout
to make assignments for two people on the cleaning crew.

STAFF DUTIES   June 1

Apartments to be	1	2	3	4	5	6	7	8	9	10
cleaned by June 2nd:	11	12	13	14	15	16	17	18	19	20
	21	22	**23**	24	25	26	27	**28**	29	**30**

Other Maintenance:
Apartment 16 needs curtains.
The carpet in apartment 14 has to be cleaned.

Employee: _Hong_

Clean these apartments: _____

Answers will vary.

Other maintenance:
Apartment # Request

Employee: _Jane_

Clean these apartments: _____

Other maintenance:
Apartment # Request

Performance Review

I can...

☐ **1.** put information in a computer.

☐ **2.** get information from a computer.

☐ **3.** understand information from a computer.

☐ **4.** use information from a computer.

Discussion

Work with a team. How will the skills help you? Make a list.
Share the list with your class.

38   Unit 3

PRESENTATION

Follow the instructions on page 37.

INFORMAL WORKPLACE-SPECIFIC ASSESSMENT

Ask learners to identify one task at
work or at home that a computer helps
them accomplish. Have them describe
how they input, get, and/or use
information to accomplish the task.

WORKBOOK

Unit 3, Exercise 9

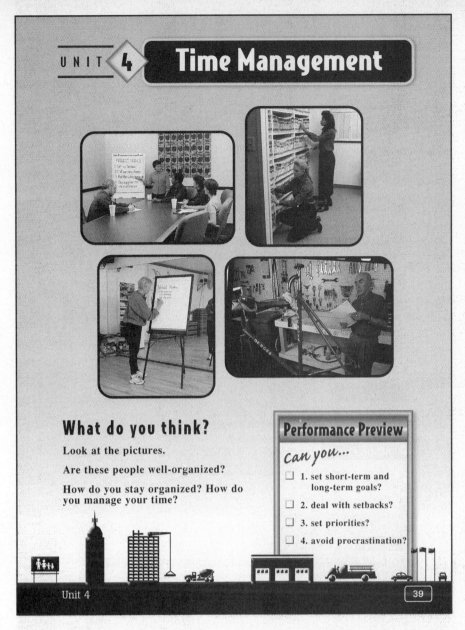

UNIT 4 — Time Management

What do you think?

Look at the pictures.

Are these people well-organized?

How do you stay organized? How do you manage your time?

Performance Preview

Can you...

- ☐ 1. set short-term and long-term goals?
- ☐ 2. deal with setbacks?
- ☐ 3. set priorities?
- ☐ 4. avoid procrastination?

Unit 4

39

Unit 4 Overview
—SCANS Competencies—

★ Allocate time

★ Select equipment and tools

★ Work on teams

★ Understand organizational systems

★ Monitor and correct performance

Workforce Skills

- Set short-term and long-term goals
- Deal with setbacks
- Set priorities
- Avoid procrastination

Materials

- Clock
- Course catalogs from local community colleges or technical schools
- Picture cards of a flat tire, wedding cake, snow, mechanics, auto technician, and wrench
- Calendar
- Work order and newspaper advice column

Unit Warm-Up

To get the learners thinking about the unit topic (setting and meeting goals) talk about your goals for the class. Tell learners your goals for this class session and the whole course. Identify these as short-term and long-term goals. Encourage learners to tell their short- and long-term goals for the class.

★　　★　　★　　★　　★

WORKFORCE SKILLS (page 39)

Set short-term and long-term goals

Set priorities

★　　★　　★　　★　　★

PREPARATION

Act out two ways of coming to class. First, set the hands of a clock to five minutes before the scheduled class time. Leave the room, and calmly reenter. Next, set the clock to five minutes after class time. Leave the room then reenter in a hurried manner. Have learners compare and contrast.

PRESENTATION

1. Focus attention on the photographs. Ask learners to speculate what the unit might be about. Write their ideas on the board and/or restate them in acceptable English.

2. Have learners talk about the photographs. Encourage them to say as much as they can about each picture. Help learners identify workplaces and describe what the employees are doing.

3. Help learners read the questions. Discuss the questions with the class.

4. You may want to use the Performance Preview to provide learners with an overview of the skills in the unit. Have learners read the list of skills and discuss what they will learn in the unit.

FOLLOW-UP

Staying Organized: Have learners brainstorm items that help people organize their work and their time, such as watches, calendars, alarm clocks, bus schedules, file drawers, and to-do lists. Write the list on the board.

◆ Have teams talk about how they use one or more of the items on the list at home or at work to stay organized. Have team reporters summarize discussions for the class.

WORKBOOK

Unit 4, Exercises 1A–1B

Teaching Note

Use this page to introduce the new language in the unit. Whenever possible, encourage peer teaching. Supply any language learners need.

SCANS Note

Explain to learners that companies generally have both long-term and short-term goals. Ask learners if they know their employers' goals or can speculate about them. Have learners share ideas about how their jobs help their employers achieve their goals.

Getting Started — Thinking about goals

READ

① I'll catch the 7:05 bus and get to work on time every day.

② I'm improving my math skills so I can apply for the assistant manager position.

③ I'm taking a lesson in flower arrangment to improve the look of the reception area at work.

④ I want to get my driver's license so I can apply for the delivery driver position.

TEAM WORK

Look at the pictures. What are the people's goals? Are they long-term goals or short-term goals? What other goals might the people have?

PARTNER WORK

Student A says a goal. Student B says whether it's a short-term goal or a long-term goal.

A I want to learn to weld.

B That sounds like a good long-term goal.

SURVEY

Do people in your class have similar goals? Ask each of your classmates to tell you one short-term and one long-term goal. Make a chart.

40   Unit 4

PREPARATION

To present or review **short-term** and **long-term** goals, follow the instructions in Unit Warm-Up on page 39.

PRESENTATION

1. Have learners read and discuss the Purpose Statement. For more information, see "Purpose Statement" on page viii.

2. Focus attention on the illustrations. Encourage learners to say as much as they can about them. Write their ideas on the board and/or restate them in acceptable English. Then have them read the captions under each picture.

3. Have teams read the Team Work instructions. Make sure each team knows what to do. If necessary, model the first item. Remind the teams that they are responsible for making sure that each member understands the new language. Then have teams complete the activity. Have team reporters share their answers with the class.

 4. Have partners read the Partner Work instructions. Make sure partners know what to do. If necessary, model the activity. Then have partners complete the activity. Have learners switch partners and repeat the activity. Have one or two partners present their dialogs to the class.

5. Have teams read the Survey instructions. Make sure each learner knows what to do. If necessary, model the activity. Then have teams complete the activity. Have teams share their answers with the class. For more information, see "Survey" on page viii.

FOLLOW-UP

How Long Will It Take? Have partners talk about how long it will take them to achieve the goals they listed in the Survey. Have several pairs share their dialogs with the class.

♦ As a class, discuss why it is important to have goals and how staying organized can help people meet their goals. Discuss why people sometimes have difficulty meeting goals.

WORKBOOK

Unit 4, Exercise 2

Talk About It Talking about your goals
....

 **PRACTICE THE DIALOG**

A You've been here for three months, and you're doing a very good job as file clerk. What are your goals for working with Uptown Paper Products?

B Well, I'd like to work in the inventory department someday.

A That's a good long-term goal. Do you have goals for the near future?

B I'd like to start learning data entry. I can sign up for a course at the learning center.

A You're headed in the right direction.

Useful Language

In the meantime, . . .

Eventually, . . .

Right now, . . .

Tip When you set a long-term goal, break it up into short-term goals. It will be easier to see your progress and accomplish your goal.

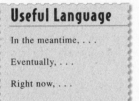 **PARTNER WORK**

Talk about long-term goals and identify short-term goals that will help you reach them. Use the dialog and the Useful Language above.

ASAP
PROJECT

As a class, make a list of long-term and short-term goals for your class. Include plans for achieving each goal. Update the list as you make progress toward your goals. Complete this project as you work through the unit.

Unit 4

`41`

ASAP
PROJECT

Have learners read the instructions. Discuss the project and its purpose with learners. Help learners assign themselves to teams based upon their knowledge, skills, interests, or other individual strengths. Have each team select a leader, and have the team leaders or the whole class select an overall project leader. Throughout the rest of the unit, allow time for learners to work on the project. Make sure that everyone understands. Have the teams agree on a deadline when the project will be finished. For more information, see "ASAP Project" on page vi.

PREPARATION

To present or review **short-term** and **long-term** goals, follow the instructions in Unit Warm-Up on page 39.

PRESENTATION

1. Have learners read and discuss the Purpose Statement. For more information, see "Purpose Statement" on page viii.

2. Focus attention on the photograph. Encourage learners to say as much as they can about it. Write their ideas on the board and/or restate them in acceptable English. Then present the dialog. See "Presenting a Dialog" on page ix.

3. Have partners read the Partner Work instructions. Make sure everyone understands what to do. Focus attention on the Useful Language box. Help learners read the expressions. If necessary, model pronunciation. Then have learners complete the activity. Have learners switch partners and repeat the activity. Have one or two pairs present their dialogs to the class.

Tip Have learners read the Tip independently. Have learners discuss why it is important to break up long-term goals into short-term goals. For more information, see "Presenting a Tip" on page ix.

FOLLOW-UP

Get a Better Job: Display course catalogs in fields that might interest learners. Ask partners to discuss how taking a course might help them get a better job in the future or advance at their current job. Have several pairs share their ideas with the class.

♦ Ask partners to talk about how they can rearrange their work and personal schedules to make time for the courses of study they chose. Have partners write notes about the changes. Ask several pairs to share their ideas with the class.

WORKBOOK

Unit 4, Exercise 3

★   ★   ★   ★   ★

Language Note

Tell learners different words for setback, such as stumbling block, hang up, obstacle, delay, and slowdown. Then discuss expressions for ways to solve a problem, such as get around a problem, think through a problem, tackle a problem, eliminate a problem, and deal or cope with a problem. Ask learners if they can add to these lists.

Personal Dictionary

Have learners add the words in their Personal Dictionary to their *Workforce Writing Dictionary.* For more information, see "Workforce Writing Dictionary" on page v.

Keep Talking — Dealing with setbacks

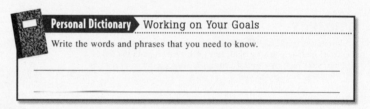

PRACTICE THE DIALOG

A I have a lot of deliveries to make, but my truck has a flat tire.

B I can help you out. What do you have to do?

A Well, first I have to take a wedding cake up to East 51 Street. That'll take 40 minutes. Then I have to deliver an order of bread to the Wild West Steak House downtown.

B I'll help you fix the flat. Then while you're delivering the cake, I can take the bread downtown.

DISCUSSION

Work with a partner. Talk about how to solve the problems in these situations. Use the dialog above.

1. You and your partner are supposed to make 100 salads, but you have only enough lettuce for 50 salads.

2. You and your partner have to make deliveries to several customers, but it's snowing very hard and it's not safe to drive.

Personal Dictionary ❯ Working on Your Goals

Write the words and phrases that you need to know.

_____

_____

42   Unit 4

PREPARATION

1. Use picture cards to clarify **flat tire, wedding cake,** and **snow.**

2. Act out a problem that will make it difficult to have class, such as a power failure. Explain that the name for this sort of problem is **setback.** Ask learners to think of solutions such as moving to a different building, rescheduling the class, or using other light sources. Write learners' ideas on the board.

PRESENTATION

1. Have learners read the Purpose Statement. For more information, see "Purpose Statement" on page viii.

2. Focus attention on the illustration. Have partners discuss the setback it presents. Then present the dialog. See "Presenting a Dialog" on page ix.

3. Have learners read the Discussion instructions. Make sure everyone knows what to do. Then have learners work in pairs to discuss solving the problems. Have several partners share their ideas with the class.

4. Have learners read the Personal Dictionary instructions. Then use the Personal Dictionary procedures on page ix. Remind learners to continue to add words to their dictionaries throughout the unit.

FOLLOW-UP

Setback and Solution: Divide the class into three teams. Assign each team one of the following setbacks: a landscape maintenance worker whose lawn mower stops working; a server who drops a plate of food on a customer's lap; an office assistant whose telephone stops working. Ask each team to agree on a solution. Have team reporters share their setbacks and solutions with the class.

♦ Have teams write a list of the steps they would take to carry out their solutions. Have team reporters share their lists with the class.

WORKBOOK

Unit 4, Exercises 4A–4B

 **Listening** | Changing priorities and dealing with setbacks

 LISTEN AND CIRCLE

These people have to change their schedules because their priorities changed. Why did their priorities change? Circle the answer in column A.

	A	B
1	(The meeting was rescheduled.) He missed the meeting. He didn't put gas in the truck.	Fill the bins first. (Make the deliveries later.) Change the meeting time.
2	Some bikes are broken. Some parts are missing. (The mechanics need to assemble the bikes.)	(Unpack the bikes first.) Sort the parts first. Call the customers first.
3	Maintenance takes half an hour. (A customer's machine doesn't work at all.) All the customers called.	Start at Priority Publishing. Start at Quality Hardware. (Start at Music House.)

 LISTEN AGAIN

How do they change their schedules? Circle the answer in column B.

 LISTEN AND CIRCLE

1. What were they planning to do today?

   a. They were planning to move the shelves.

   (b.) They were planning to have a sidewalk sale.

2. What is the setback that makes them change their plans?

   a. The paper didn't run their ad.

   (b.) There is a big storm coming.

3. How did they change their plans to deal with the setback?

   (a.) They will move the shelves so they can have the sale inside.

   b. They will cancel the sale.

Unit 4

43

Set priorities

Deal with setbacks

★　　★　　★　　★　　★

SCANS Note

Tell learners that two important aspects of problem-solving are **creativity** *and* **flexibility.** *People who think creatively about a setback use their imaginations to resolve it. People who approach a problem with flexibility change priorities to accommodate it. Ask learners for concrete examples of creativity and flexibility at their workplaces.*

PREPARATION

1. To teach or review **setback,** follow procedures on page 42. To teach or review **priorities,** ask learners to tell you some things that are very important to them and some that are less important. Write the items on the board. Identify the most important ones as their priorities.

2. Use picture cards and/or pantomime to present or review **maintenance, mechanics, assemble,** and **unpack.**

PRESENTATION

1. Have learners read and discuss the Purpose Statement. For more information, see "Purpose Statement" on page viii.

 2. Have learners read the Listen and Circle instructions. Make sure that everyone knows what to do. If necessary, model the first item. Then play the tape or read the Listening Transcript aloud two or more times as learners complete the activity. Have learners check their work. For more information, see "Presenting a Listening Activity" on page ix.

 3. Have learners read the Listen Again instructions. Then follow the procedures in 2.

4. Have learners read the Listen and Circle instructions. Then follow the procedures in 2.

FOLLOW-UP

Set Back the Clock: Tell learners to imagine that they are an hour behind at work because of a problem earlier in the day. Have them discuss with a partner the best way to cope with the situation. Ask several partners to share their dialogs with the class.

◆ Have partners write a list of ways they could cope with the problem of getting lost on the way to a job interview. Have partners share their lists with the class.

WORKBOOK

Unit 4, Exercises 5A–5B

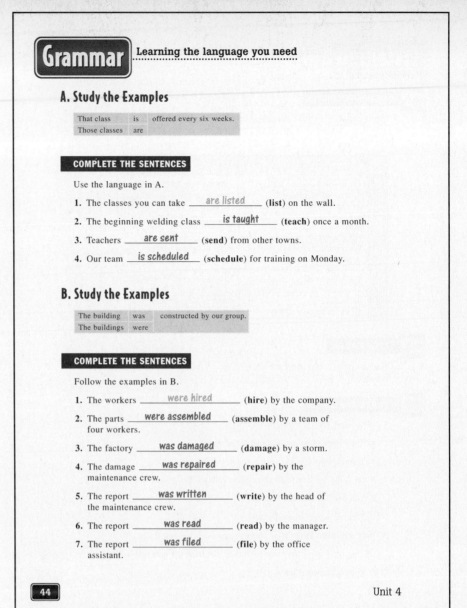

Grammar
Learning the language you need

A. Study the Examples

| That class | is | offered every six weeks. |
| Those classes | are | |

COMPLETE THE SENTENCES

Use the language in A.

1. The classes you can take ___are listed___ (**list**) on the wall.
2. The beginning welding class ___is taught___ (**teach**) once a month.
3. Teachers ___are sent___ (**send**) from other towns.
4. Our team ___is scheduled___ (**schedule**) for training on Monday.

B. Study the Examples

| The building | was | constructed by our group. |
| The buildings | were | |

COMPLETE THE SENTENCES

Follow the examples in B.

1. The workers ___were hired___ (**hire**) by the company.
2. The parts ___were assembled___ (**assemble**) by a team of four workers.
3. The factory ___was damaged___ (**damage**) by a storm.
4. The damage ___was repaired___ (**repair**) by the maintenance crew.
5. The report ___was written___ (**write**) by the head of the maintenance crew.
6. The report ___was read___ (**read**) by the manager.
7. The report ___was filed___ (**file**) by the office assistant.

44   Unit 4

PREPARATION

Review the language in the grammar boxes with learners before they open their books, if necessary. Use pantomime to present or review **assembled, damaged,** and **repaired.**

PRESENTATION

1. Have learners read and discuss the Purpose Statement. For more information, see "Purpose Statement" on page viii.

2. Have learners read the grammar box in A. Have learners use the language in the box to say as many sentences as possible. Tell learners that they can use the grammar boxes throughout the unit to review or check sentence structures.

3. Focus attention on Complete the Sentences. Make sure learners know what to do. If necessary, model the first item. Then have learners complete the activity independently. Ask several learners to read their sentences aloud while the rest of the class checks their work.

4. Focus attention on the grammar box in B. Follow the procedures in 2.

5. Focus attention on Complete the Sentences. Follow the procedures in 3.

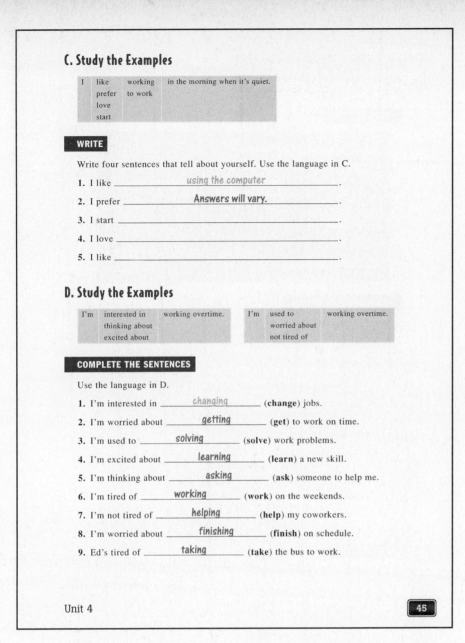

C. Study the Examples

I	like	working	in the morning when it's quiet.
	prefer	to work	
	love		
	start		

WRITE

Write four sentences that tell about yourself. Use the language in C.

1. I like _____ *using the computer* _____.

2. I prefer _____ Answers will vary. _____.

3. I start _____.

4. I love _____.

5. I like _____.

D. Study the Examples

I'm	interested in	working overtime.		I'm	used to		working overtime.
	thinking about				worried about		
	excited about				not tired of		

COMPLETE THE SENTENCES

Use the language in D.

1. I'm interested in _____ *changing* _____ (**change**) jobs.

2. I'm worried about _____ *getting* _____ (**get**) to work on time.

3. I'm used to _____ *solving* _____ (**solve**) work problems.

4. I'm excited about _____ *learning* _____ (**learn**) a new skill.

5. I'm thinking about _____ *asking* _____ (**ask**) someone to help me.

6. I'm tired of _____ *working* _____ (**work**) on the weekends.

7. I'm not tired of _____ *helping* _____ (**help**) my coworkers.

8. I'm worried about _____ *finishing* _____ (**finish**) on schedule.

9. Ed's tired of _____ *taking* _____ (**take**) the bus to work.

Unit 4

45

---

6. Focus attention on the grammar box in C. Follow the procedures in 2.

7. Have learners read the instructions for Write. If necessary, model the first item. Then have learners complete the activity independently. Ask several learners to read their sentences aloud.

8. Focus attention on the grammar boxes in D. Follow the procedures in 2.

9. Focus attention on Complete the Sentences. Follow the procedures in 3.

FOLLOW-UP

What I Like: Have partners create dialogs about what they like doing at work. Have learners take turns talking about their long-term goals based on the parts of their jobs they enjoy the most. Ask several pairs to present their dialogs to the class.

♦ Have learners identify three short-term goals they need to pursue to complete their long-term goals. Ask learners to share their ideas with the class.

WORKBOOK

Unit 4, Exercises 6A–6D

BLACKLINE MASTERS

Blackline Master: Unit 4

★   ★   ★   ★   ★

SCANS Note

Explain to learners that employees' priorities might not always be the same as those of their employers. For instance, an employee might want to leave an unpleasant task until the end of the day. However, the employer might want that task done right away. Ask learners why employees should give their employers' priorities more importance than their own when they are at work.

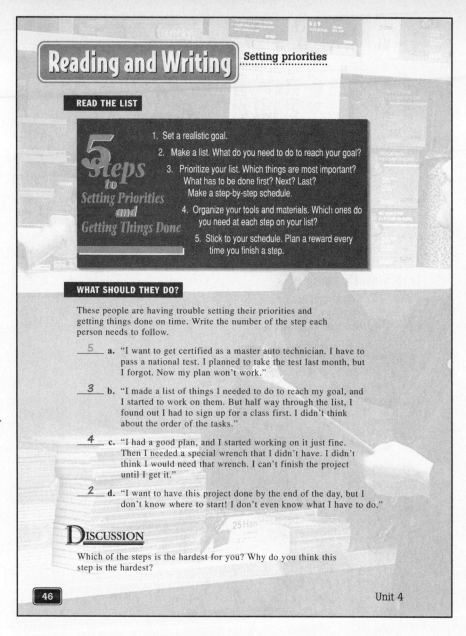

PREPARATION

1. Use realia, pictures, or role-play to teach or review **auto technician** and **wrench.**

2. To present or review **prioritize,** follow the procedures in Preparation on page 43. Then explain that **prioritize** means "to list items in order, beginning with the most important item." Ask learners to prioritize the items on the board.

PRESENTATION

1. Have learners read and discuss the Purpose Statement. For more information, see "Purpose Statement" on page viii.

2. Have learners preview the list of steps before they read. See "Prereading"

on page x. Encourage learners to say everything they can about the list. Write their ideas on the board and/or restate them in acceptable English. Then have them read the list independently.

3. Have learners read the instructions for What Should They Do? Make sure everyone knows what to do. Model the first item if necessary. Then have learners complete the activity independently. Ask several partners to share their answers with the class while the rest of the class checks their work.

4. Have learners read the Discussion instructions. Make sure everyone knows what to do. Then have learners work in teams to discuss their responses to the questions. Have team reporters share responses with the class.

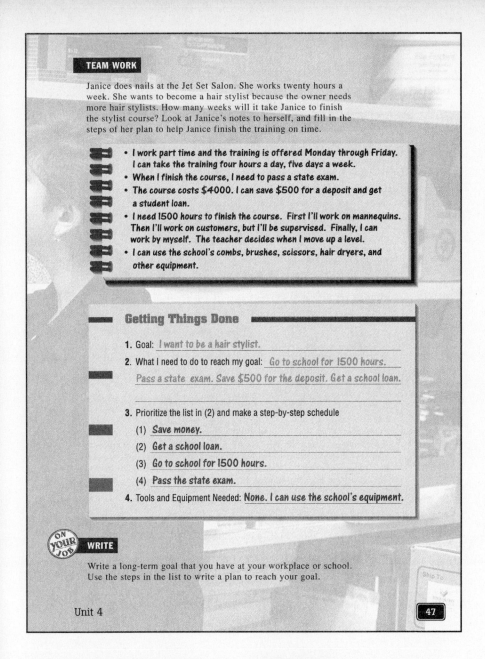

TEAM WORK

Janice does nails at the Jet Set Salon. She works twenty hours a week. She wants to become a hair stylist because the owner needs more hair stylists. How many weeks will it take Janice to finish the stylist course? Look at Janice's notes to herself, and fill in the steps of her plan to help Janice finish the training on time.

- • I work part time and the training is offered Monday through Friday. I can take the training four hours a day, five days a week.
- • When I finish the course, I need to pass a state exam.
- • The course costs $4000. I can save $500 for a deposit and get a student loan.
- • I need 1500 hours to finish the course. First I'll work on mannequins. Then I'll work on customers, but I'll be supervised. Finally, I can work by myself. The teacher decides when I move up a level.
- • I can use the school's combs, brushes, scissors, hair dryers, and other equipment.

Getting Things Done

1. Goal: <u>I want to be a hair stylist.</u>

2. What I need to do to reach my goal: <u>Go to school for 1500 hours.</u>
   <u>Pass a state exam. Save $500 for the deposit. Get a school loan.</u>

3. Prioritize the list in (2) and make a step-by-step schedule
   (1) <u>Save money.</u>
   (2) <u>Get a school loan.</u>
   (3) <u>Go to school for 1500 hours.</u>
   (4) <u>Pass the state exam.</u>

4. Tools and Equipment Needed: <u>None. I can use the school's equipment.</u>

WRITE

Write a long-term goal that you have at your workplace or school. Use the steps in the list to write a plan to reach your goal.

Unit 4 — 47

---

5. Have learners preview the realia on the page. Follow the procedures in 2.

6. Have teams read the Team Work instructions. Make sure each team knows what to do. If necessary, model the first item. Remind the teams that they are responsible for making sure each member understands the new language. Then have teams complete the activity. If learners need help, encourage them to consult other teams. Have team reporters share their answers with the class.

 7. Have learners read the instructions for Write. Make sure everyone knows what to do. If necessary, model the activity. Then have learners complete the activity. Have several learners share their goals and plans with the class.

FOLLOW-UP

Schedules: Have partners work together to assess how long it will take each partner to achieve the long-term goal he or she identified in Write. Then have them consult a calendar and add a completion date next to each item in the step-by-step schedule. Have a few volunteers present their schedules to the class.

♦ Have partners identify the step on each schedule they think will be hardest to complete. Ask them to discuss possible rewards for those steps. Have several pairs summarize their discussions for the class.

WORKBOOK

Unit 4, Exercises 7A–7B

★　　　★　　　★　　　★　　　★

SCANS Note

You might discuss the impact of one employee's procrastination on others. Ask learners for examples of procrastination at work that had a negative impact on more than one employee.

 **Extension** ········ **Avoiding procrastination**

ANSWER THE QUESTIONS

Read the article and talk about it with a partner. What's procrastination? What are some reasons that people procrastinate? Why does Jamie procrastinate about filing the work orders? What's the solution to Jamie's problem?

Avoiding Procrastination

Many people procrastinate—they put things off. If you procrastinate at work, you should correct the problem before it gets worse. Some people procrastinate to avoid jobs that they don't like. Others put off things that they are afraid to do. What's Jamie's problem in the following story?

The Work Isn't Getting Done. Jamie works in the office of a large apartment complex. Everyone likes Jamie because she is very helpful. Jamie contacts the maintenance department immediately to report problems. She writes work orders for the maintenance team right away, but she puts off filing the orders when the work is done.

Mrs. Macon, the manager, decided to help Jamie get organized. She asked Jamie why the work orders hadn't been filed. Jamie explained that she always runs out of time. She also admitted that she doesn't like filing. Mrs. Macon had

noticed that Jamie spends a lot of time talking to the residents to help them solve their problems. Mrs. Macon suggested that every day Jamie should file the previous day's work orders first thing in the morning. That way, Jamie can get the job she doesn't like out of the way so it won't interrupt the part of the job that she likes to do.

 ***Culture*Notes**

How do you avoid procrastinating at your workplace or school? How do you reward yourself for doing a job well?

PREPARATION

1. To clarify the meaning of **procrastination,** role-play a food server who notices that there is not very much ice at the beverage station but puts off getting more ice. Describe what you are doing and thinking. Then act out running out of ice at a busy moment.

2. Use pictures, realia, and/or pantomime to present or review **avoid, work order, filing,** and **interrupt.**

PRESENTATION

1. Have learners read and discuss the Purpose Statement. For more information, see "Purpose Statement" on page viii.

2. Have learners preview the article before they read. See "Prereading" on page x. Encourage them to say everything they can about the article. Write their ideas on the board and/or restate them in acceptable English. Then have learners read the article independently.

3. Have learners read the instructions for Answer the Questions. Make sure everyone knows what to do. Then have learners work in teams to discuss the article and answer the questions. Have team reporters share their answers with the class.

4. Have learners read Culture Notes and talk over their responses in teams. Have team reporters share their ideas with the class. Ask the teams to compare each other's ideas. See "Culture Notes," page vii.

FOLLOW-UP

Procrastination Counselor: Have partners role-play a meeting between a person who procrastinates and a counselor who gives advice on preventing the problem. Have partners switch roles and repeat the activity. Ask several pairs to present their dialogs to the class.

◆ Have partners write their dialogs in the form of a letter and response in a newspaper advice column. Provide a sample advice column for students to use as a model. Post the letters and responses.

WORKBOOK

Unit 4, Exercise 8

Performance Check | How well can you use the skills in this unit?

Complete the activities. Go over your work with a partner or your teacher. Then complete the Performance Review on page 50.

SKILL 1 | **SET SHORT-TERM AND LONG-TERM GOALS**

Tell your partner or teacher about one short-term goal and one long-term goal that you would like to achieve.

SKILL 2 | **DEAL WITH SETBACKS**

Talk with a partner or your teacher. Solve these problems.

1. You are in charge of serving lunch to a group of visitors to your company. You were planning to serve lunch on the patio, but it's raining outside.

2. You need to deliver a wedding cake this afternoon, but the truck won't start.

SKILL 3 | **SET PRIORITIES**

Will I Finish on Time?

1. Set a realistic goal.
2. Make a list.
3. Prioritize your list and make a step-by-step plan.
4. Organize your tools.
5. Stay on schedule and reward yourself at every step.

What do these people need to do to manage their time better? Look at the chart, and write the number of the step they need to follow.

__4__ **a.** "Look at this mess! I have a list of what I need to do, but I can't find my hammers or wrenches."

__3__ **b.** "I made a list, but it doesn't help. I don't know what to do first."

__5__ **c.** "I never finish anything because in the middle of the project it doesn't seem like fun anymore. Even though I know exactly what I'm supposed to do, I have trouble doing it. There's no reward."

Unit 4

49

PRESENTATION

Use any of the procedures in "Evaluation," page x, with pages 49 and 50. Record individuals' results on the Unit 4 Individual Competency Chart. Record the class's results on the Class Cumulative Competency Chart.

STOP Procrastinating

Many people procrastinate or put off things they need to do. They often find that the problem doesn't go away by itself. One solution is to set aside time each day to do the tasks you don't like. Marco describes how this helped him in his job as a cashier at a hair salon. "I enjoyed talking to the customers, but I would put off organizing the stylists' receipts. I tried setting aside five minutes every hour to go through the receipts. It worked. Now I can still talk to the customers and always leave knowing that my job is done."

Read the article and talk over the questions with a partner or your teacher.

1. What task did Marco procrastinate about?

2. What is the solution to Marco's problem?

Performance Review

I can...

☐ 1. set short-term and long-term goals.

☐ 2. deal with setbacks.

☐ 3. set priorities.

☐ 4. avoid procrastination.

DISCUSSION

Work with a team. How will the skills help you? Make a list. Share the list with your class.

50   Unit 4

PRESENTATION

Follow the instructions on page 49.

INFORMAL WORKPLACE-SPECIFIC ASSESSMENT

Have learners explain to you how they can manage their time better. Ask questions about setting goals, dealing with setbacks, prioritizing, and avoiding procrastination if necessary.

WORKBOOK

Unit 4, Exercise 9

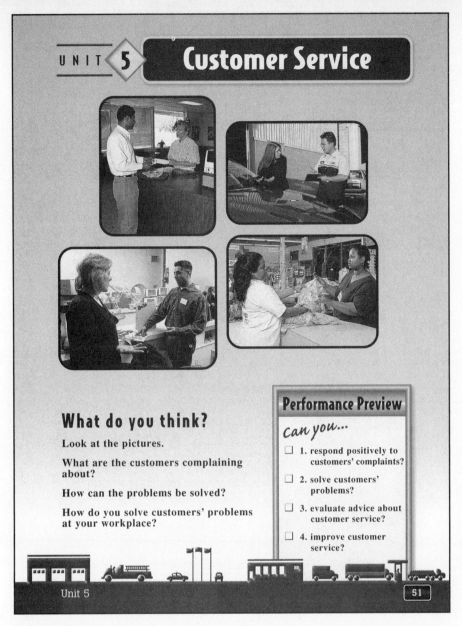

UNIT 5 Customer Service

What do you think?

Look at the pictures.

What are the customers complaining about?

How can the problems be solved?

How do you solve customers' problems at your workplace?

Performance Preview

Can you...

☐ 1. respond positively to customers' complaints?

☐ 2. solve customers' problems?

☐ 3. evaluate advice about customer service?

☐ 4. improve customer service?

Unit 5   51

★ Serve customers

★ Interpret and communicate information

★ Solve problems

★ Improve systems

Workforce Skills

● Respond positively to customers' complaints

● Solve customers' problems

● Evaluate advice about customer service

● Improve customer service

Materials

● Picture cards or realia of a tile; popcorn; ants; grass; weeds; holes; an alarm; tree clippings; a power saw; an invoice; an answering machine and tape; a certificate from a hotel, car rental company, or airline

● Brochures from a car rental agency and an apartment complex

● Blank customer suggestion forms

Unit Warm-Up

To get the learners thinking about the unit topic (working with customers), ask learners to brainstorm positive and negative responses to customers, for example *smiles* and *acts rude*. Write their ideas on the board.

★   ★   ★   ★   ★

WORKFORCE SKILLS (page 51)

Respond positively to customers' complaints

PREPARATION

Ask learners if they have ever complained about a product or service. What was the problem? Who did they complain to? What happened?

PRESENTATION

1. Focus attention on the photographs. Ask learners what they think the unit is about. Write their ideas on the board and/or restate them in acceptable English.

2. Have learners talk about the photos. Help them identify the workplaces and the products the people are talking about.

3. Help learners read the questions. Discuss the questions with the class.

4. You may want to use the Performance Preview to provide learners with an overview of the skills in the unit. Have learners read the list of skills and discuss what they will learn in the unit.

FOLLOW-UP

Good Customer Service: Have partners select one of the photographs on this page. Ask them to create two dialogs about the situation. In the first dialog, have partners model poor customer service. In the second, have them model good customer service. Ask several partners to present their dialogs to the class.

◆ Have pairs write the second dialog. Ask them to underline the key phrases that indicate good customer service. Have learners share their ideas with the class.

WORKBOOK

Unit 5, Exercises 1A–1B

WORKFORCE SKILLS (page 52)

Respond positively to customers' complaints

Solve customers' problems

★　　★　　★　　★　　★

Teaching Note

Use this page to introduce the new language in the unit. Whenever possible, encourage peer teaching. Supply any language learners need.

SCANS Note

Suggest that dealing with customers' complaints is just one way to provide good service. Other ways include offering a quality product and providing on-time service. Ask learners for more ideas and write them on the board.

Getting Started

Responding to customers' complaints

TEAM WORK

Look at the pictures. Each employee is dealing with a customer's complaint. How does each employee respond? Can you think of other responses?

> a. I'm sorry. I'll clean this up right away.
>
> b. I apologize. Here's some popcorn with no butter.
>
> c. Please accept my apology. I'll replace the tile immediately.

This tile is cracked. __c__

I think that you spilled some trash. __a__

I think I ordered popcorn with no butter. __b__

PARTNER WORK

Your partner tells you about one of the problems above. Apologize and offer a solution.

A This tile is cracked.

B I'm sorry. I can replace it for you.

 Tip Customers usually want fast solutions. If you can't solve a problem right away, apologize and explain why.

SURVEY

Write down a customer service problem you have experienced at your workplace. Survey your classmates to find out how they would solve it. How was the problem really solved? Share everyone's ideas and the real solution with the class.

52

Unit 5

PREPARATION

1. To present or review **apologize,** act out apologizing to a customer. List phrases people commonly use when they apologize.

2. Use realia or picture cards to present or review **tile** and **popcorn.** Use pantomime to review **replace.**

PRESENTATION

1. Have learners read and discuss the Purpose Statement. See "Purpose Statement" on page viii.

2. Focus attention on the illustrations. Encourage learners to say as much as they can about them. Write their ideas on the board and/or restate them in acceptable English.

3. Have teams read the Team Work instructions and complete the activity.

Have team reporters share their answers with the class.

4. Have partners read the Partner Work instructions and complete the activity. Have one or two pairs present their dialogs to the class.

 5. Have learners read the Survey instructions and complete the activity. Have learners share their answers with the class.

Tip Have learners read the Tip independently and discuss how the advice will help them. See "Presenting a Tip" on page ix.

FOLLOW-UP

Bar Graph: Make a table on the board with the following headings: **Refund, Replace, Substitute,** and **Redo.** Help

the class tally the number of learners who have used each method to solve a customer service problem. Write the totals on the table.

◆ Help teams create bar graphs that show the information in the table. The horizontal axis should show the methods of solving service problems; the vertical axis should show the number of learners who have used each method. For more information, see page viii. Post the graphs in the classroom.

WORKBOOK

Unit 5, Exercise 2A–2B

Respond positively to customers' complaints

Solve customers' problems

★   ★   ★   ★   ★

Talk About It   Meeting customers' needs

 PRACTICE THE DIALOG

A   Able Pest Control. How may I help you?

B   Hi, this is Maria Delano. You treated my house for ants last week, and the ants are already back.

A   I'm sorry, we've had a lot of rain lately, so it's hard to keep the ants out. I'll send someone to your house again, free of charge.

B   Thanks a lot. I appreciate it.

PARTNER WORK

Your partner has the following customer service problem. You help solve the problem. Use the dialog above.

> Three days ago, Green Lawns Service came to cut the grass and pull weeds. There are tall weeds on the lawn already. Ask the workers to come back.

ASAP
PROJECT

Work with a team. Prepare a customer service manual for a business everybody knows, such as a grocery store. Include policies on dealing with different customer complaints, such as bad food, products that don't work, items that are sold out, etc. Complete this project as you work through the unit.

Unit 5   53

ASAP
PROJECT

Have learners read the instructions. Discuss the project and its purpose with learners. Make sure that everyone understands. Help learners assign themselves to teams based upon their knowledge, skills, interests, or other individual strengths. Have each team select a leader. Throughout the rest of the unit, allow time for learners to work on the project. Have the teams agree on a deadline when the project will be finished. For more information, see "ASAP Project" on page vi.

PREPARATION

1. To present or review **free of charge,** act out giving free merchandise to a customer in response to a customer service problem. Ask learners if they have ever been given anything free of charge.

2. Use picture cards to present or review **ants, grass, lawn,** and **weeds.**

PRESENTATION

1. Have learners read and discuss the Purpose Statement. For more information, see "Purpose Statement" on page viii.

 2. Focus attention on the illustration. Encourage learners to say as much as they can about it. Ask them what the customer might be complaining about.

Then present the dialog. See "Presenting a Dialog" on page ix.

3. Have partners read the Partner Work instructions. Make sure everyone understands what to do. Then have learners complete the activity. Have learners switch partners and repeat the activity. Have one or two pairs present their dialogs to the class.

FOLLOW-UP

Dialogs: Have partners choose a problem in one of the following categories: **bad service, bad food,** or **bad product.** Have partners create dialogs in which one acts as a customer with the problem and the other acts as an employee who deals with the problem. Have pairs present their dialogs to the class.

♦ Have partners write their dialogs. Check their work.

WORKBOOK

Unit 5, Exercise 3

★   ★   ★   ★   ★

SCANS Note

Explain that learners should be clear about how much they can do when solving customer service problems. For example, many employees do not have the authority to offer refunds or exchanges. Suggest that learners speak to their supervisors if they aren't clear about the limits of their authority.

Language Note

*Develop a list of phrases learners can use to give customers explanations for service problems such as **because, so, as a result of,** and **caused by.** Provide examples, such as "The delivery was late because of a flat tire."*

Personal Dictionary

Have learners add the words in their Personal Dictionary to their *Workforce Writing Dictionary*. For more information, see "Workforce Writing Dictionary" on page v.

Keep Talking — Solving customers' problems

PRACTICE THE DIALOG

A Hi, Ms. Haines. Welcome back. Did you decide you wanted to rent apartment 306 after all?

B I'm still not sure. I liked the apartment, but I'd rather not live on the third floor. I don't want to climb all those stairs.

A There's a similar apartment available on the first floor, but the kitchen is a little smaller. Would you like to see it?

B Sure, if you can show it to me right away. I have to be back at work in 20 minutes.

PARTNER WORK

Have you ever had a customer come to you with a problem? How did you solve the problem? Was the customer satisfied? Discuss these questions with your partner.

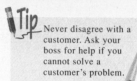

Tip Never disagree with a customer. Ask your boss for help if you cannot solve a customer's problem.

Personal Dictionary ▸ Providing Solutions for Customers

Write the words and phrases that you need to know.

_____

_____

_____

54   Unit 5

PREPARATION

Use a picture card or a brochure from an apartment complex to present or review **apartment** and **rent.**

PRESENTATION

1. Have learners read the Purpose Statement. For more information, see "Purpose Statement" on page viii.

 2. Focus attention on the photograph. Have partners talk about who the people are and what they might be saying. Then present the dialog. See "Presenting a Dialog" on page ix.

3. Have partners read the Partner Work instructions. Make sure everyone understands what to do. Then have learners complete the activity. Have

learners switch partners and repeat the activity. Have one or two pairs present their dialogs to the class.

4. Have learners read the Personal Dictionary instructions. Then use the Personal Dictionary procedures on page ix. Remind learners to continue to add words to their dictionaries throughout the unit.

Tip Have learners read the Tip independently and discuss how the advice will help them. For more information, see "Presenting a Tip" on page ix.

FOLLOW-UP

Let Me Make Sure I Understand:
Have learners work in pairs to create dialogs in which a customer describes a problem and an employee restates the

customer's complaint. Encourage learners to use problems they have dealt with at their workplaces. Have several partners present their dialogs to the class.

♦ Have teams discuss how to explain a customer service problem to a supervisor when the customer is present. Have team reporters share their teams' ideas with the class.

WORKBOOK

Unit 5, Exercise 4

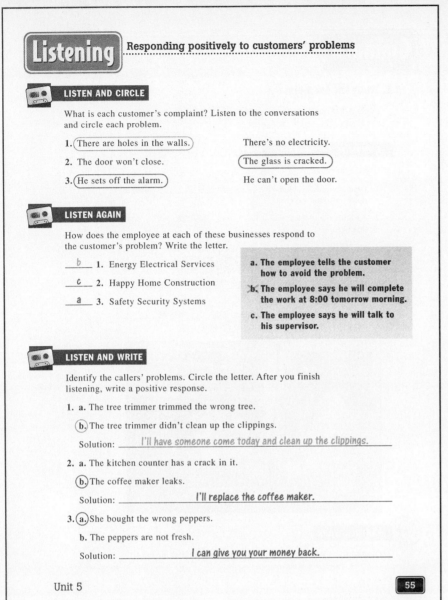

Listening — Responding positively to customers' problems

LISTEN AND CIRCLE

What is each customer's complaint? Listen to the conversations and circle each problem.

1. (There are holes in the walls.)   There's no electricity.

2. The door won't close.   (The glass is cracked.)

3. (He sets off the alarm.)   He can't open the door.

LISTEN AGAIN

How does the employee at each of these businesses respond to the customer's problem? Write the letter.

__b__ 1. Energy Electrical Services

__c__ 2. Happy Home Construction

__a__ 3. Safety Security Systems

> a. The employee tells the customer how to avoid the problem.
>
> b. The employee says he will complete the work at 8:00 tomorrow morning.
>
> c. The employee says he will talk to his supervisor.

LISTEN AND WRITE

Identify the callers' problems. Circle the letter. After you finish listening, write a positive response.

1. a. The tree trimmer trimmed the wrong tree.

   (b.) The tree trimmer didn't clean up the clippings.

   Solution: ___I'll have someone come today and clean up the clippings.___

2. a. The kitchen counter has a crack in it.

   (b.) The coffee maker leaks.

   Solution: ___I'll replace the coffee maker.___

3. (a.) She bought the wrong peppers.

   b. The peppers are not fresh.

   Solution: ___I can give you your money back.___

Unit 5   [55]

PREPARATION

Use picture cards, explanation, realia, and pantomime to present or review **holes, alarm, cracked, tree trimmer,** and **clippings.**

PRESENTATION

1. Have learners read and discuss the Purpose Statement. For more information, see "Purpose Statement" on page viii.

 2. Have learners read the Listen and Circle instructions. Make sure everyone knows what to do. If necessary, model the first item. Then play the tape or read the Listening Transcript aloud two or more times as learners complete the activity. Have learners check their work. For more information, see "Presenting a Listening Activity" on page ix.

 3. Have learners read the Listen Again instructions. Then follow the procedures in 2.

 4. Have learners read the Listen and Write instructions. Then follow the procedures in 2.

FOLLOW-UP

Negative and Positive: Have learners work in pairs. Ask partners to choose one problem discussed on this page and role-play an employee handling the customer's complaint in a negative manner, then in a positive manner. Have several pairs present their role-plays to the class.

♦ Have teams discuss situations in which an employee is not able to solve a customer's problem. Encourage learners to use situations that might occur at their workplaces. How can the employees handle the situations positively? When should they call in a supervisor? Have teams share their ideas.

SCANS Note

Explain that companies value a positive attitude not only in customer service, but in every aspect of employees' jobs. Discuss ways people demonstrate a positive attitude.

WORKBOOK

Unit 5, Exercises 5A–5B

Respond positively to customers' complaints

Solve customers' problems

Improve customer service

★　　★　　★　　★　　★

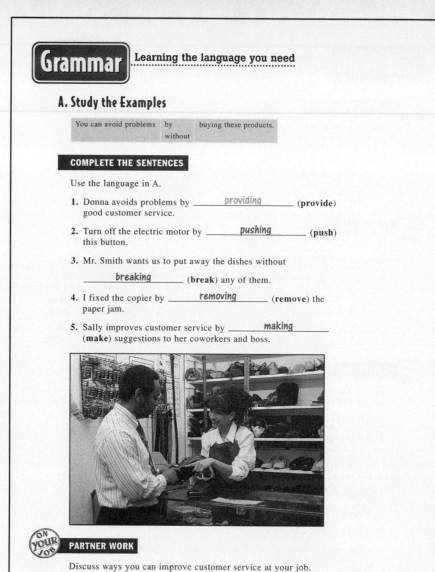

| Grammar | Learning the language you need |

A. Study the Examples

| You can avoid problems | by without | buying these products. |

COMPLETE THE SENTENCES

Use the language in A.

1. Donna avoids problems by _____providing_____ (**provide**) good customer service.

2. Turn off the electric motor by _____pushing_____ (**push**) this button.

3. Mr. Smith wants us to put away the dishes without _____breaking_____ (**break**) any of them.

4. I fixed the copier by _____removing_____ (**remove**) the paper jam.

5. Sally improves customer service by _____making_____ (**make**) suggestions to her coworkers and boss.

 PARTNER WORK

Discuss ways you can improve customer service at your job.

PREPARATION

1. Review the language in the grammar box with learners before they open their books, if necessary.

2. Use realia or picture cards to present or review **power saw** and **invoice**.

PRESENTATION

1. Have learners read and discuss the Purpose Statement. For more information, see "Purpose Statement" on page viii.

2. Have learners read the grammar box in A. Have learners use the language in the box to say as many sentences as possible. Tell learners that they can use the grammar box throughout the unit to review or check sentence structures.

3. Focus attention on Complete the Sentences. If necessary, model the first item. Then have learners complete the activity independently. Have a different learner read each sentence aloud as the rest of the class checks their answers.

 4. Have partners read the Partner Work instructions. Make sure everyone knows what to do. If necessary, model the activity with a learner. Then have partners complete the activity. Have learners switch partners and repeat the activity. Ask several partners to present their dialogs to the class.

B. Study the Examples

I sent it	by	train.
		mail.
		mistake.

| I did it | with | a pen. |
| | without | |

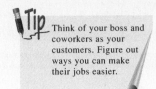

Tip Think of your boss and coworkers as your customers. Figure out ways you can make their jobs easier.

COMPLETE THE SENTENCES

Use *by*, *with*, or *without*.

1. I started the truck _____*with*_____ the spare key.

2. We got to the work site _____*by*_____ bus.

3. Phil painted the walls _____*with*_____ gray paint.

4. He's sending the supplies _____*by*_____ mail.

5. The job was hard because I did it _____*without*_____ a power saw.

6. Amanda sends invoices _____*by*_____ fax.

7. They received that delivery _____*by*_____ mistake.

8. He finished the project by himself. He did it _____*without*_____ help.

9. The customer wants extra French fries _____*with*_____ his hamburger.

10. At Discount Office Supplies you can order _____*by*_____ telephone.

COMPLETE THE SENTENCES

Use the language in A and B.

1. The crew finished the job without ____*staying late*____.

2. Alice shipped the boxes by ____*Answers will vary.*____.

3. They are cutting down the tree with _____.

4. Ed can pack those boxes without _____.

5. We're going to fix the problem by _____.

6. You should always chop the vegetables with _____.

7. You can't make hamburgers without _____.

Unit 5

57

Language Note

*Explain to learners that some words have positive or negative connotations. To illustrate, discuss with learners the different meanings suggested by **cheap** and **less expensive**. Tell learners that it is important to use words with positive connotations when dealing with customers.*

---

5. Focus attention on the grammar boxes in B. Follow the procedures in 2.

6. Have learners read the instructions for Complete the Sentences. Follow the procedures in 3.

7. Have learners read the instructions for Complete the Sentences. Follow the procedures in 3.

Tip Have learners read the Tip independently. Have learners discuss ways they can make their supervisors' and coworkers' jobs easier. For more information, see "Presenting a Tip" on page ix.

FOLLOW-UP

Happy Customers: Write this sentence starter on the board: *I can provide good customer service by _____.*
Have partners take turns repeating the

sentence as they fill in the blank with phrases such as "smiling" or "demonstrating how the vacuum cleaner works." Encourage learners to complete the sentences with examples from their own workplaces. Ask several learners to say their sentences for the class.

♦ Ask learners to write their sentences. Check their work.

WORKBOOK

Unit 5, Exercises 6A–6C

BLACKLINE MASTERS

Blackline Master: Unit 5

★　★　★　★　★

Reading and Writing Improving customer service

READ THE CUSTOMER SERVICE GUIDELINES

DIAL Customer Service Guidelines
Telephone Store

a. Listen to the customer's complaint and apologize for the problem.

b. Think over the customer's complaint and figure out the reason for the problem.

c. Solve the problem. Talk to your supervisor if you can't find a solution.

d. Thank the customer.

e. Report the complaint and your solution to your boss.

WRITE THE LETTER

Read what the employees at Dial Telephone Store said. Write the letter of the guideline that each employee is using.

__a__ 1. I'm sorry that your new answering machine isn't working.

__c__ 2. I'll get you a new tape for your answering machine.

__d__ 3. Thank you for bringing that to our attention. We appreciate your business.

__b__ 4. Your answering machine isn't working because the tape is broken.

__e__ 5. Mr. Valdez, a customer brought in a new answering machine with a broken tape. I replaced the tape for her.

__b__ 6. We've had some trouble with these answering machines. Sometimes the tape breaks.

__c__ 7. I think I'll have to talk to my boss about that. I'm not sure what our policy is, but we'll find a solution as soon as possible.

PARTNER WORK

You work at Dial Telephone Store. Your partner is a customer whose new telephone isn't working. Solve the problem. Follow the guidelines.

58　　　　　　　　　　　　　　　　　　　　Unit 5

Culture Note

Explain to learners that companies like employees to give "service with a smile." However, it is usually not appropriate to smile while a customer is making a complaint.

PREPARATION

Use realia or picture cards to identify an **answering machine** and **tape.** Ask learners to describe problems they've had with answering machines.

PRESENTATION

1. Have learners read and discuss the Purpose Statement. For more information, see "Purpose Statement" on page viii.

2. Have learners preview the guidelines before they read. See "Prereading" on page x. Encourage learners to say everything they can about the guidelines. Write their ideas on the board and/or restate them in acceptable English. Then have them read the guidelines independently.

3. Have learners read the instructions for Write the Letter. Make sure everyone knows what to do. Model the first item if necessary. Then have learners complete the activity independently. Have learners review each other's work as partners. Then ask learners to read their answers aloud while the rest of the class checks their work.

4. Have partners read the Partner Work instructions. Make sure everyone understands what to do. Model if necessary. Then have learners complete the activity. Have learners switch partners and repeat the activity. Have several partners present their dialogs to the class.

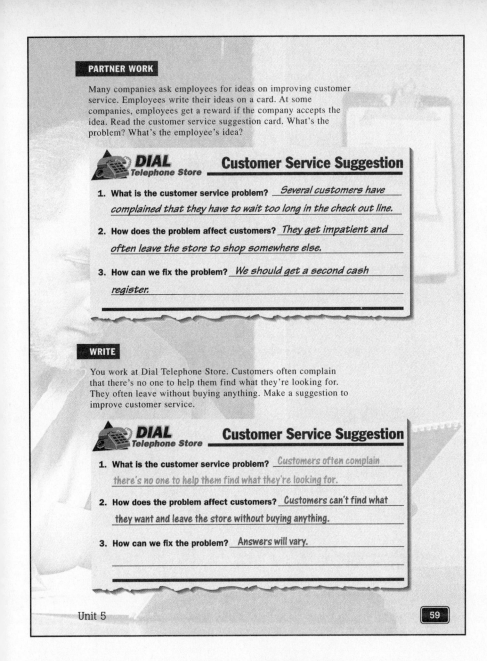

Many companies ask employees for ideas on improving customer service. Employees write their ideas on a card. At some companies, employees get a reward if the company accepts the idea. Read the customer service suggestion card. What's the problem? What's the employee's idea?

DIAL Telephone Store **Customer Service Suggestion**

1. **What is the customer service problem?** *Several customers have complained that they have to wait too long in the check out line.*

2. **How does the problem affect customers?** *They get impatient and often leave the store to shop somewhere else.*

3. **How can we fix the problem?** *We should get a second cash register.*

WRITE

You work at Dial Telephone Store. Customers often complain that there's no one to help them find what they're looking for. They often leave without buying anything. Make a suggestion to improve customer service.

DIAL Telephone Store **Customer Service Suggestion**

1. **What is the customer service problem?** *Customers often complain there's no one to help them find what they're looking for.*

2. **How does the problem affect customers?** *Customers can't find what they want and leave the store without buying anything.*

3. **How can we fix the problem?** *Answers will vary.*

Unit 5

59

5. Have learners preview the customer service suggestion card. Follow the procedures in 2.

6. Have partners read the Partner Work instructions. Make sure everyone understands what to do. Then have learners complete the activity. Have learners switch partners and repeat the activity. Have one or two partners present their ideas to the class.

7. Have learners read the instructions for Write. Make sure each learner knows what to do. If necessary, model the activity. Then have learners complete the activity. Have several learners share their suggestions with the class.

FOLLOW-UP

Suggest a Solution: Provide learners with blank Customer Service Suggestion forms. Ask them to complete the forms by making suggestions for improving customer service at their workplaces. Have learners read their completed forms to the class.

◆ Have partners exchange completed forms and talk about additional ways to solve the customer service problem. Ask several learners to share their ideas with the class.

WORKBOOK

Unit 5, Exercises 7A–7C

Extension · Following advice about customer service

READ THE DIALOG

It was very busy today at Airport Car Rentals, and they ran out of luxury cars. They only have economy cars in the lot.

A What do we do if a customer ordered a luxury car?

B Well, say you're sorry and tell the customer you'll deduct $5 per day from the cost of the economy car.

A What if the customer's upset?

B Offer the customer a certificate for a free upgrade on their next rental.

PARTNER WORK

Read the situations. Which customers get free upgrade certificates? Tell why.

1. Mr. Manning reserved the most expensive luxury car. When Mr. Manning found out he couldn't get a luxury car, he became angry.

2. Ms. Rush reserved an economy car, but she wants a luxury car. There are only economy cars on the lot.

3. Ms. Lozano reserved a luxury car. When she found out there were only economy cars, she didn't seem annoyed.

 *Culture Notes*

What do you do at your workplace if a customer is angry or rude?
What do you say when you can't do what a customer wants?

60   Unit 5

PREPARATION

1. Use a brochure from a car rental agency to present or review **rental, luxury, economy**, and **upgrade.**

2. Display and identify a **certificate** for a discount or upgrade from a hotel, car rental company, or airline. Ask learners where they've seen such certificates before.

PRESENTATION

1. Have learners read and discuss the Purpose Statement. See "Purpose Statement" on page viii.

2. Focus attention on the illustration. Help learners identify the workplace. Ask what the speakers might be saying. Then have learners read the dialog independently.

3. Have partners read the Partner Work instructions. Model if necessary. Then have learners complete the activity. Have a few learners present their ideas to the class.

 4. Have learners read Culture Notes and talk over their responses in teams. Have teams share ideas. See "Culture Notes," page vii.

FOLLOW-UP

Asking for Advice: Have learners take turns asking a partner for advice about a problem at work or at school. As the partner responds, have learners ask one or two follow-up questions to clarify the advice. Allow learners to use imaginary problems if they wish. Have several pairs present their conversations to the class.

♦ Have teams discuss giving advice about customer service to colleagues. Should they give advice if it isn't asked for? Should they give advice if they aren't sure about company policy? Should they follow-up to make sure their advice is taken? Have team reporters summarize the ideas for the class.

WORKBOOK

Unit 5, Exercise 8

Complete the activities. Go over your work with a partner or your teacher.
Then complete the Performance Review on page 62.

SKILL 1   RESPOND POSITIVELY TO CUSTOMERS' COMPLAINTS

What is the customer's complaint? Listen and circle.

a. The refrigerator isn't cold.

b. The refrigerator is damaged.

How would you respond to the customer's request? Circle the letter.

a. Tell her it's not your fault the refrigerator is damaged.

b. Offer to deliver a new refrigerator.

SKILL 2   SOLVE CUSTOMERS' PROBLEMS

You are a customer service representative at a department store.
Your partner or teacher ordered a couch three weeks ago, but still
hasn't received it. Tell your partner or teacher how you would
solve the problem.

SKILL 3   EVALUATE ADVICE ABOUT CUSTOMER SERVICE

Read the conversation. Decide which customer gets a luxury
room tomorrow night. Tell why.

A Mr. Jones, all our rooms are occupied, but several guests with
reservations are still coming.

B Yes, sometimes that happens. Usually we send them to the Shady
Grove Hotel next door.

A What happens if they're upset?

B Tell them that tomorrow night you'll put them in a special luxury
room here.

1. Ellen arrived at 11:30 at night. She had a reservation. She
was upset when she found out she had to go to the Shady
Grove Hotel.

2. Tim arrived at 4:30 in the afternoon without a reservation.
He was sent to the Shady Grove Hotel. He didn't complain.

Unit 5

61

PRESENTATION

Use any of the procedures in
"Evaluation," page x, with pages 61 and
62. Record individuals' results on the
Unit 5 Individual Competency Chart.
Record the class's results on the Class
Cumulative Competency Chart.

You work at Classic Home Furniture. Customers often complain that the delivery drivers arrive late. They are annoyed because they have to wait a long time for deliveries. Sometimes they are late to work because they have to wait at home. Use the form to make a suggestion for improving customer service.

Classic Home Furniture **Customer Service Suggestion**

1. What is the customer service problem? _Customers often complain that the delivery drivers are late._

2. How does the problem affect customers? _Customers get angry because they have to stay at home waiting for the delivery drivers._

3. How can we fix the problem? _Answers will vary._

_____

Performance Review

I can...

☐ 1. respond positively to customers' complaints.

☐ 2. solve customers' problems.

☐ 3. evaluate advice about customer service.

☐ 4. improve customer service.

DISCUSSION

Work with a team. How will the skills help you? Make a list. Share the list with your class.

Unit 5

PRESENTATION

Follow the instructions on page 61.

INFORMAL WORKPLACE-SPECIFIC ASSESSMENT

Ask learners to explain how they can solve customer service problems at their workplace in a positive manner. If learners do not interact with customers, have them explain how they can respond positively to coworkers' or supervisors' problems.

WORKBOOK

Unit 5, Exercise 9

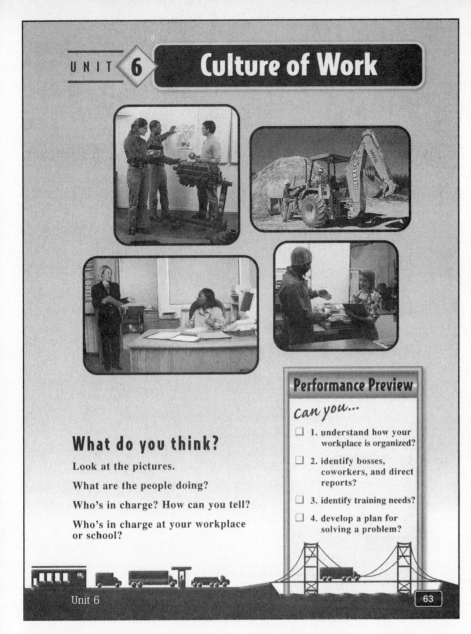

UNIT 6 — Culture of Work

What do you think?

Look at the pictures.

What are the people doing?

Who's in charge? How can you tell?

Who's in charge at your workplace or school?

Performance Preview

can you...

☐ 1. understand how your workplace is organized?

☐ 2. identify bosses, coworkers, and direct reports?

☐ 3. identify training needs?

☐ 4. develop a plan for solving a problem?

Unit 6 Overview
—SCANS Competencies—

★ Understand organizational systems

★ Communicate information

★ Work on teams

★ Allocate staff

★ Design and improve systems

Workforce Skills

● Understand how your workplace is organized

● Identify bosses, coworkers, and direct reports

● Identify training needs

● Develop a plan for solving a problem

Materials

● Picture cards of employees at work, a service garage, a construction site, a parking lot

● Mail-order catalogs for office supplies or other products; list of a company's training classes

Unit Warm-Up

To get learners thinking about the unit topic (workplace organization), draw an organizational chart for your school on the board. Discuss with learners why it is important to know who your bosses are.

★　★　★　★　★

WORKFORCE SKILLS (page 63)

Identify bosses, coworkers, and direct reports

★　★　★　★　★

PREPARATION

1. Present or review **boss, coworker, and direct report.** Use the organizational chart developed in the Warm-Up activity to clarify meanings. Encourage learners to use the new language as they talk about the organization of their workplaces.

2. Ask learners to talk about the responsibilities of a boss at their workplace. How is the boss's job different from that of the other workers?

PRESENTATION

1. Focus attention on the photographs. Ask learners to say what they think the unit is about. Write their ideas on the board and/or restate them in acceptable English.

2. Have learners talk about the photographs. Help them identify the workplaces and describe each worker's role.

3. Help learners read the questions. Discuss the questions with the class.

4. You may want to use the Performance Preview to provide learners with an overview of the skills in the unit. Have learners read the list of skills and discuss what they will learn in the unit.

FOLLOW-UP

Company Organization: Have learners work in teams. Give each team a picture that shows employees at work. Ask teams to describe the workplace, say what the people are doing, and decide if the employees are coworkers or if one is a boss. Ask team reporters to summarize their ideas for the class.

♦ Tell partners to imagine they've walked into a workplace for the first time. What clues would tell them which person is in charge? Ask team reporters to share their ideas with the class.

WORKBOOK

Unit 6, Exercise 1

Teaching Note

Use this page to introduce the new language in the unit. Whenever possible, encourage peer teaching. Supply any language learners need.

SCANS Note

Explain that if an employee wants to move up to a higher position at work, it can help to understand the organization of the workplace. If workers understand the responsibilities of other employees, they can identify the training and experience required for a better job. Ask learners to talk about skills they would need if they had their boss's job.

Getting Started
Understanding how your workplace is organized

PARTNER WORK

Look at the people in the picture. Who are the supervisors? How do you know?

TEAM WORK

Match the letter of the job with the sentence that person might say.

| a. manager | b. cashier | c. mechanic | d. mechanic's assistant |

_a_ 1. "The mechanic and the cashier report to me."

_c_ 2. "I repair and maintain the motorcycles we sell."

_d_ 3. "I help the mechanic."

_b_ 4. "I run the register and help customers. I report to the manager."

PARTNER WORK

Talk about how each person contributes to the workplace.

A What does the manager do?

B The manager supervises the employees.

 SURVEY

Work with a team. Ask team members to say how many bosses they work with regularly at their workplaces or schools. Make a table.

64   Unit 6

PREPARATION

Use a picture card of a service garage to present or review **mechanic** and **mechanic's assistant.** Explain that **repair** means "fix a problem," and **maintain** means "keep something in good working condition."

PRESENTATION

1. Have learners read and discuss the Purpose Statement. See "Purpose Statement" on page viii.

2. Focus attention on the illustration. Encourage learners to say as much as they can about it. Write learners' ideas on the board and/or restate them in acceptable English.

3. Focus attention on Partner Work and have learners complete the activity. Have learners share their ideas with the class.

4. Have teams read the Team Work instructions. Make sure each team knows what to do. If necessary, model the first item. Then have teams complete the activity. If learners need help, encourage them to consult other teams. Have team reporters share the answers with the class.

5. Have partners read the Partner Work instructions. Make sure partners know what to do. Then have them complete the activity. Have several partners share their ideas with the class.

 6. Have learners read the Survey instructions. Make sure each learner knows what to do. Then have teams complete the activity. Have teams display their tables. For more information, see "Survey" on page viii.

FOLLOW-UP

Pie Chart: Help the class tally the information from the Survey and use it to create a pie chart showing the percentage of learners who work with different numbers of bosses. Have learners discuss the chart. For more information, see "Survey" on page viii.

♦ Have partners talk about the ideal number of bosses. Do they prefer to report to one boss or more than one boss? Why? Have several pairs summarize their ideas for the class.

WORKBOOK

Unit 6, Exercises 2A–2B

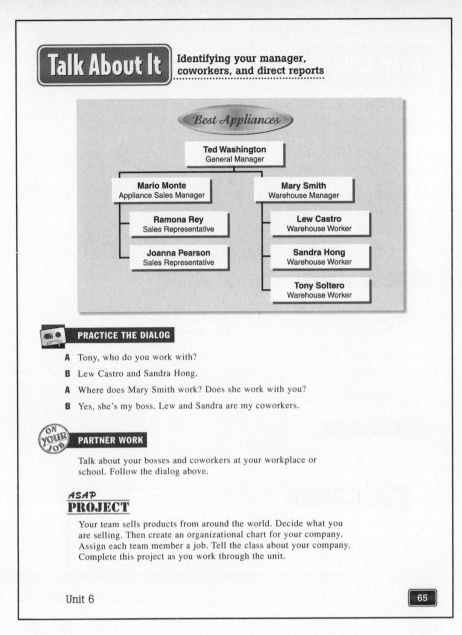

Talk About It
Identifying your manager, coworkers, and direct reports

Best Appliances

Ted Washington — General Manager

Mario Monte — Appliance Sales Manager
- **Ramona Rey** — Sales Representative
- **Joanna Pearson** — Sales Representative

Mary Smith — Warehouse Manager
- **Lew Castro** — Warehouse Worker
- **Sandra Hong** — Warehouse Worker
- **Tony Soltero** — Warehouse Worker

PRACTICE THE DIALOG

A Tony, who do you work with?

B Lew Castro and Sandra Hong.

A Where does Mary Smith work? Does she work with you?

B Yes, she's my boss. Lew and Sandra are my coworkers.

PARTNER WORK

Talk about your bosses and coworkers at your workplace or school. Follow the dialog above.

ASAP PROJECT

Your team sells products from around the world. Decide what you are selling. Then create an organizational chart for your company. Assign each team member a job. Tell the class about your company. Complete this project as you work through the unit.

Unit 6   65

Understand how your workplace is organized

Identify bosses, coworkers, and direct reports

★　　★　　★　　★　　★

ASAP PROJECT

Have learners read the instructions. Discuss the project and its purpose with learners. Make sure that everyone understands. Help learners assign themselves to teams based upon their knowledge, skills, interests, or other individual strengths. Throughout the rest of the unit, allow time for learners to work on the project. Have the teams agree on a deadline when the project will be finished. For more information, see "ASAP Project" on page vi.

Language Note

*Review with learners different titles a boss may have, such as **supervisor, manager, superintendent, team leader,** and **foreman.** Ask learners what titles bosses have at their workplaces.*

PREPARATION

1. To present or review **manager, boss, coworker,** and **direct report,** follow the instructions in Preparation on page 63.

2. Ask learners to name the person or persons they report to at work. Who does their boss report to? Encourage learners to use the words **manager, direct report,** and **coworker** in their answers.

PRESENTATION

1. Have learners read and discuss the Purpose Statement. For more information, see "Purpose Statement" on page viii.

2. Focus attention on the organizational chart. Encourage learners to say as much as they can about it. Ask them to explain who reports to who. Then present the dialog. See "Presenting a Dialog" on page ix.

3. Have partners read the Partner Work instructions. Make sure everyone understands what to do. Then have learners complete the activity. Have learners switch partners and repeat the activity. Have one or two pairs present their dialogs to the class.

FOLLOW-UP

Job Responsibilities: Have partners talk about the job responsibilities of the employees on the organizational chart on the Student Book page. Ask several partners to present their dialogs to the class.

♦ Divide the class into two teams. Have one team say the name of a managerial job, such as "restaurant manager." Then have the other team name employees who probably directly report to that manager, such as "dishwasher," "food server," and "host" or "hostess." Continue, having teams take turns naming the managerial job.

WORKBOOK

Unit 6, Exercises 3A–3C

WORKFORCE SKILLS (page 66)

Understand how your workplace is organized

Identify bosses, coworkers, and direct reports

Culture Note

Tell learners that if they have a problem at work, they should not discuss it with their boss's supervisor before talking to their own boss. If possible, workers should always tell their boss about a problem first. (Exceptions include sexual harassment involving the boss and emergency situations.) Explain that people appreciate being given the chance to solve a problem before their supervisor knows about it. Ask learners why they think this is so.

Personal Dictionary

Have learners add the words in their Personal Dictionary to their *Workforce Writing Dictionary*. For more information, see "Workforce Writing Dictionary" on page v.

Keep Talking Talking about the organization of your workplace

 PRACTICE THE DIALOG

A What does Harmony Music do?

B Harmony Music is a distributor that sells music CDs to businesses and individuals. Our goal is to locate CDs that are hard to find.

A It sounds like an interesting place to work. How many employees are there?

B There are five of us. Our customers call in orders or contact us by mail. Barry's in charge of shipping the orders. I'm responsible for sales.

 PARTNER WORK

Tell your partner about the company you work for. Explain your role at the company. Follow the dialog above.

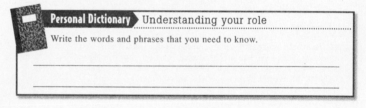

Personal Dictionary Understanding your role

Write the words and phrases that you need to know.

_____

_____

66   Unit 6

PREPARATION

To present or review the new language on the page, display a mail-order catalog. Explain that the company is a **distributor.** It provides products to customers who **contact,** or communicate with, the company's **sales** staff to place orders. The **shipping** department sends out the products.

PRESENTATION

1. Have learners read the Purpose Statement. See "Purpose Statement" on page viii.

 2. Focus attention on the illustration. Have learners say everything they can about it. Write their ideas on the board and/or restate them in acceptable English.

Then present the dialog. See "Presenting a Dialog" on page ix.

 3. Have partners read the Partner Work instructions. Model the activity if necessary. Make sure everyone knows what to do. Then have learners complete the activity. Have learners switch partners and repeat the activity. Have several pairs present their dialogs to the class.

4. Have learners read the Personal Dictionary instructions. Then use the Personal Dictionary procedures on page ix. Remind learners to continue to add words to their dictionaries throughout the unit.

FOLLOW-UP

Higher Up: Have one partner tell the other about a supervisor's job where he or she works. Who are the supervisor's direct reports? What does the supervisor do? Have partners switch roles and repeat. Ask several pairs to present their dialogs to the class.

♦ Have partners help each other make an organizational chart for each partner's workplace. Post the charts in the classroom.

WORKBOOK

Unit 6, Exercise 4

English ASAP

Listening　Solving problems

LISTEN AND CIRCLE

The people are solving problems. Listen to the conversations. Answer the questions.

Conversation 1

1. Why did the supervisor call the meeting?

    a. She wants to hire another worker.

    (b.) She wants Luis's and Craig's suggestions.

2. What does Luis think they need?

    (a.) another carpenter

    b. another construction team

3. Who does Craig suggest?

    (a.) a former employee

    b. another construction company

4. Why is Vince a good suggestion?

    (a.) Because he has experience.

    b. Because he will be available in a few months.

> **Tip** Always take notes at meetings. Note-taking helps you remember important decisions.

Conversation 2

1. What do workers do when they can't find parking spaces?

    (a.) They park on the grass.

    b. They park behind other cars in the factory lot.

2. What's their first idea on how to solve the problem?

    (a.) Workers can park at the school.

    b. Workers can park down the street.

3. Why won't the suggestion work?

    a. Workers have to pay to park there.

    (b.) Parking is by permit only.

DISCUSSION

How can the employees solve the parking problem in Conversation 2? Share your ideas with the class.

Unit 6　67

PREPARATION

Use a picture card of a construction site to present or review **carpenter** and **construction.** Use a picture card of a parking lot to preteach **parking spaces** and **paved.**

PRESENTATION

1. Have learners read and discuss the Purpose Statement. See "Purpose Statement" on page viii.

 2. Have learners read the Listen and Circle instructions. If necessary, model the first item. Then play the tape or read the Listening Transcript aloud two or more times as learners complete the activity. Have learners check their work. See "Presenting a Listening Activity" on page ix.

3. Have learners read the Discussion question. Then have learners work in teams to discuss their ideas. Have team reporters share ideas with the class.

> **Tip** Have learners read the Tip independently and discuss how the advice will help them. See "Presenting a Tip" on page ix.

FOLLOW-UP

Make a Suggestion: Have learners brainstorm a list of phrases they can use when making suggestions at work. If learners need help getting started, suggest possibilities such as, "I have an idea," or "I think there might be a way

to avoid that problem." Write learners' ideas on the board.

♦ Have learners work in pairs to create dialogs in which one coworker describes a problem at work and the other suggests a solution. Have partners switch roles and repeat the activity. Ask several pairs to present their dialogs to the class.

WORKBOOK

Unit 6, Exercise 5

Understand how your workplace is organized

Identify training needs

Develop a plan for solving a problem

★   ★   ★   ★   ★

SCANS Note

*Encourage learners to memorize the "Five W's"—**who, what, where, when,** and **why**—in the grammar box in A. Tell learners they can use these words to ask questions about confusing tasks or projects at work.*

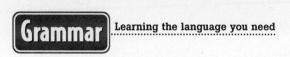

Grammar   Learning the language you need

A. Study the Examples

> Who's in charge of the shipping department?
> What's she in charge of?
> Where's the manager's office?
> When's the delivery going to arrive?
> Why's there a police car in the parking lot?

COMPLETE THE DIALOG

Use the language in A.

A _____ *Who*'s in charge of installing the new washing machines?

B I am.

A _____ *When* _____ are we going to start the work?

B At 11:00. We'll probably finish at about 3:00.

A _____ *Why* _____ will the work take four hours?

B Because we're going to install several machines.

A _____ *Where* _____ are the machines now?

B In the break room. I'll see you there at 11:00.

 TEAM WORK

Take turns asking questions about each teammate's workplace or school. Are the workplaces organized the same way? How are they the same? How are they different? Why? Use the language in A.

B. Study the Examples

> I read the memo. The memo was on the table.
> I read the memo that was on the table.

> I hired a mechanic. The mechanic used to work for Friendly Car Repair.
> I hired a mechanic who used to work for Friendly Car Repair.

68   Unit 6

PREPARATION

Review the language in the grammar boxes with learners before they open their books, if necessary.

PRESENTATION

1. Have learners read and discuss the Purpose Statement. For more information, see "Purpose Statement" on page viii.

2. Have learners read the grammar box in A. Have learners use the language in the box to say as many sentences as possible. Tell learners that they can use the grammar box throughout the unit to review or check sentence structures.

3. Focus attention on Complete the Dialog. If necessary, model the first item. Then have learners complete the activity independently. Ask different pairs of learners to read two lines of dialog aloud while the rest of the class checks their answers.

 4. Have teams read the Team Work instructions. Make sure each team knows what to do. If necessary, model the activity. Then have teams complete the activity. If learners need help, encourage them to consult other teams. Have team reporters share their team's answers with the class.

5. Focus attention on the grammar boxes in B. Follow the procedures in 2.

COMPLETE THE SENTENCES

Use the language in B.

1. Miguel cooked the food. The food was on the table.

   Miguel cooked the food _____*that*_____ was on the table.

2. Mr. Aziz taught a class. The class helped us fill out insurance forms.

   Mr. Aziz taught a class _____*that*_____ helped us fill out
   insurance forms.

3. I talked to a customer. The customer had some suggestions.

   I talked to a customer _____*who*_____ had some suggestions.

4. Chen has a partner. Chen's partner is a welder.

   Chen has a partner _____*who*_____'s a welder.

5. We need a secretary. The secretary speaks Spanish.

   We need a secretary _____*who*_____ speaks Spanish.

COMPLETE THE DIALOG

Write *that* or *who*.

A We have to set up a training session on using the new cash

registers _____*that*_____ we're getting next week.

B We need to find a cashier _____*who*_____ can train employees
on the new cash registers.

A Elsa is a cashier _____*who*_____ has experience on that model
cash register.

B You're right. She worked for a company _____*that*_____ had the
same registers.

A We also need a room _____*that*_____ has an electrical outlet
near a table.

B What about the meeting room _____*that*_____'s on the second floor?

A We're all set for the training session.

Unit 6

---

6. Focus attention on Complete the Sentences. If necessary, model the first item. Then have learners complete the activity independently. Ask several learners to read their sentences aloud while the rest of the class checks their answers.

7. Focus attention on Complete the Dialog and follow the procedures in 3.

FOLLOW-UP

Five Questions: Give each team a mail-order catalog. Ask teams to write five questions about the catalog or the products, using **who, what, where, when,** and **why** from the grammar box in A. Have team reporters share their questions with the class.

♦ Have team members work in pairs. Ask them to create dialogs that ask and answer the questions their team wrote about the catalog and its products. Have several pairs present their dialogs to the class.

WORKBOOK

Unit 6, Exercises 6A–6B

BLACKLINE MASTERS

Blackline Master: Unit 6

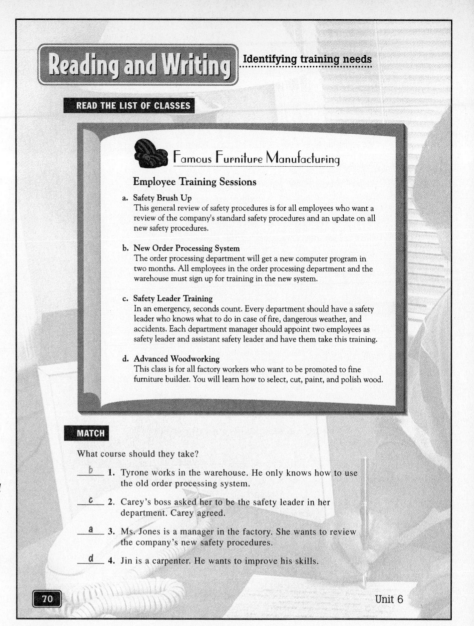

Reading and Writing
Identifying training needs

READ THE LIST OF CLASSES

Famous Furniture Manufacturing

Employee Training Sessions

a. Safety Brush Up
This general review of safety procedures is for all employees who want a review of the company's standard safety procedures and an update on all new safety procedures.

b. New Order Processing System
The order processing department will get a new computer program in two months. All employees in the order processing department and the warehouse must sign up for training in the new system.

c. Safety Leader Training
In an emergency, seconds count. Every department should have a safety leader who knows what to do in case of fire, dangerous weather, and accidents. Each department manager should appoint two employees as safety leader and assistant safety leader and have them take this training.

d. Advanced Woodworking
This class is for all factory workers who want to be promoted to fine furniture builder. You will learn how to select, cut, paint, and polish wood.

MATCH

What course should they take?

_b_ **1.** Tyrone works in the warehouse. He only knows how to use the old order processing system.

_c_ **2.** Carey's boss asked her to be the safety leader in her department. Carey agreed.

_a_ **3.** Ms. Jones is a manager in the factory. She wants to review the company's new safety procedures.

_d_ **4.** Jin is a carpenter. He wants to improve his skills.

70   Unit 6

SCANS Note

Brainstorm with learners the many different ways to get training, such as on-site company classes, courses at local technical schools or community colleges, on-the-job training, and independent study of a book or technical manual. Discuss learners' experiences with these training opportunities.

PREPARATION

1. Review or present **procedures** by role-playing a supervisor discussing safety procedures on a job. Ask learners to describe safety procedures at their work sites.

2. Explain that a worker is **promoted** when he or she receives a job at a higher level.

3. Pass around lists of training classes offered at local companies. Ask learners why some companies offer free training to their employees. Have volunteers tell where they received training to do their jobs.

PRESENTATION

1. Have learners read and discuss the Purpose Statement. For more information, see "Purpose Statement" on page viii.

2. Have learners preview the list of training courses before they read. See "Prereading" on page x. Encourage learners to say everything they can about the courses. Write their ideas on the board and/or restate them in acceptable English. Then have them read the list independently.

3. Have learners read the instructions and sentences under Match. Make sure everyone knows what to do. If necessary, model the first item. Then have learners complete the activity independently. Have partners review each other's work. Ask several pairs to share their answers with the class while the rest of the class checks their work.

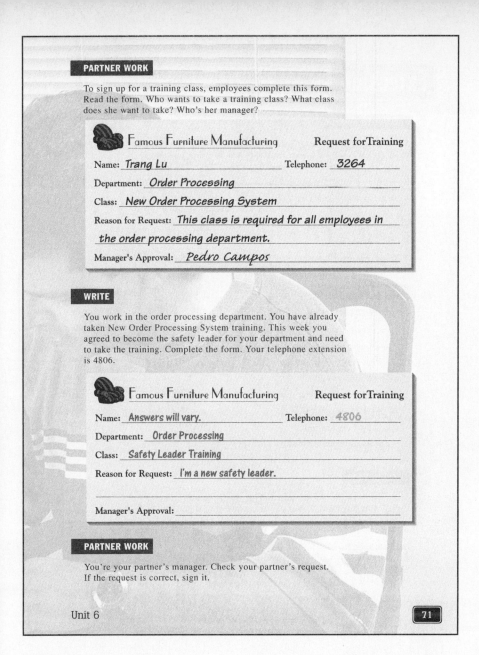

PARTNER WORK

To sign up for a training class, employees complete this form. Read the form. Who wants to take a training class? What class does she want to take? Who's her manager?

Famous Furniture Manufacturing Request for Training

Name: *Trang Lu*   Telephone: *3264*

Department: *Order Processing*

Class: *New Order Processing System*

Reason for Request: *This class is required for all employees in the order processing department.*

Manager's Approval: *Pedro Campos*

WRITE

You work in the order processing department. You have already taken New Order Processing System training. This week you agreed to become the safety leader for your department and need to take the training. Complete the form. Your telephone extension is 4806.

Famous Furniture Manufacturing Request for Training

Name: *Answers will vary.*   Telephone: *4806*

Department: *Order Processing*

Class: *Safety Leader Training*

Reason for Request: *I'm a new safety leader.*

Manager's Approval: _____

PARTNER WORK

You're your partner's manager. Check your partner's request. If the request is correct, sign it.

Unit 6   71

---

4. Have learners preview the Request for Training form. Follow the procedures in 2.

5. Have partners read the Partner Work instructions. Make sure everyone understands what to do. Model if necessary. Then have learners complete the activity. Have one or two pairs present their answers to the class.

6. Have learners read the instructions for Write. Make sure everyone knows what to do. If necessary, model the activity. Then have learners complete the activity. Have several learners share their completed forms with the class.

7. Have partners read the Partner Work instructions. Make sure everyone knows what to do. Model if necessary by reviewing and signing a learner's form. Then have learners complete the

activity. Have several partners present their signed and completed forms to the class.

FOLLOW-UP

Training Request: Display a catalog or list of training classes offered at a local company. Have partners create a dialog in which an employee requests permission from a supervisor to take one of the classes. Have learners explain why they want to take the class and how it will help them do their jobs. Have several pairs present their dialogs to the class.

♦ Have partners discuss how to sign up for and take the class they chose. Do they need to complete a registration form? Will they need special supplies, safety gear, equipment, or books? Have partners share their ideas with the class.

WORKBOOK

Unit 6, Exercises 7A–7B

Extension — Developing a plan to solve a problem

READ THE DIALOG

A   Mr. Warner, we're running a month behind schedule building the apartments on Bank Street. We had to wait for some building materials to arrive.

B   What do you think we should do?

A   Well, I asked around, and some workers can work overtime for the next few weeks. We can get back on schedule that way.

B   How long will it take?

A   About three weeks.

B   Good. I'll get Bill to start making the overtime schedule.

CIRCLE THE LETTER

1. What's Roberto worried about?
   a. The project is over budget.
   (b.) Construction is behind schedule.

2. What is the cause of the problem?
   (a.) Building materials did not arrive.
   b. They need another foreman.

3. What do they decide to do?
   a. Wait until spring.
   (b.) Pay workers overtime.

TEAM WORK

Imagine that Mr. Warner finds out the company can't afford to pay workers overtime. Make an alternative plan. Talk about it with your team members.

 **Culture Notes**

How can you request additional training at your workplace or school? Are there training opportunities where you work or study?

72   Unit 6

Culture Note

*Discuss the frequently used terms **Plan A** and **Plan B**. Explain to learners that **Plan A** is the original plan. **Plan B** is an alternate plan in case the first plan does not work. Ask volunteers to describe situations in which they had a Plan A and a Plan B. Did they use the Plan B? Why is it smart to have an alternative plan?*

PREPARATION

To present or review **schedule, overtime,** and **alternative plan,** use the words as you act out a problem at a workplace, such as a special shipment arriving one day before a sale begins. Ask learners to use the new language in sentences about problems they've had at work.

PRESENTATION

1. Have learners read and discuss the Purpose Statement. See "Purpose Statement" on page viii.

2. Have learners preview the dialog before they read. Have them count the number of exchanges, figure out how many people are talking, and skim the dialog to figure out what the people are talking about. Write their ideas on the board and/or restate them in acceptable English. See "Prereading" on page x. Then have learners read the dialog independently.

3. Have learners read the Circle the Letter instructions. Make sure everyone knows what to do. If necessary, model the first item on the board. Then have learners complete the activity independently. Have a few learners share their answers with the class.

4. Have teams read the Team Work instructions. Make sure each team knows what to do. Then have teams complete the activity. If learners need help, encourage them to consult other teams. Have team reporters share their answers with the class.

 5. Have learners read Culture Notes and talk over their responses in teams. Have team reporters share their ideas with the class. Ask the teams to compare each other's ideas. See "Culture Notes" on page vii.

FOLLOW-UP

Problems at Work: Have learners brainstorm a list of situations that can disrupt plans at work, such as bad weather, broken equipment, and sick employees. Write learners' ideas on the board.

♦ Have learners work in pairs. Ask them to choose one of the situations on the board, and have them imagine it happened at their workplace. Ask pairs to create plans that will solve the problem. Have several pairs present their plans to the class.

WORKBOOK

Unit 6, Exercises 8A–8B

 **Performance Check** | How well can you use the skills in this unit?

Complete the activities. Go over your work with a partner or your teacher.
Then complete the Performance Review on page 74.

SKILL 1 | **UNDERSTAND HOW YOUR WORKPLACE IS ORGANIZED**

What does the company you work for do? Explain your role.
Tell a partner or your teacher.

SKILL 2 | **IDENTIFY BOSSES, COWORKERS, AND DIRECT REPORTS**

Look at the organizational chart and answer the questions.

1. Who reports to Jane Goodman? _____ Jamie Salazar and Emily Walton _____

2. Who does Jay Chin report to? _____ Tim Nishimura _____

3. How many people work at The Bicycle Spoke? _____ 11 _____

4. Who is the assistant manager? _____ Jonathan Loren _____

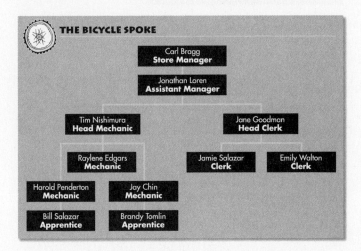

THE BICYCLE SPOKE

- Carl Bragg — **Store Manager**
- Jonathan Loren — **Assistant Manager**
- Tim Nishimura — **Head Mechanic**
- Jane Goodman — **Head Clerk**
- Raylene Edgars — **Mechanic**
- Jamie Salazar — **Clerk**
- Emily Walton — **Clerk**
- Harold Penderton — **Mechanic**
- Jay Chin — **Mechanic**
- Bill Salazar — **Apprentice**
- Brandy Tomlin — **Apprentice**

Unit 6 · 73

PRESENTATION

Use any of the procedures in
"Evaluation," page x, with pages 73 and
74. Record individuals' results on the
Unit 6 Individual Competency Chart.
Record the class's results on the Class
Cumulative Competency Chart.

Read the training options. Then read about the people. Write the name of the class each person should take.

Electronic Toys, Inc.

Training Classes

1. Office Machines Training. This class is required for all clerical help. Other employees may take the training if space permits. We will learn how to operate and make simple repairs to the fax machine, the photocopy machine, and the printer.

2. Being a Team Member. All employees must take this course. We will practice teamwork, customer service as a team, and efficient working strategies.

1. Ana Chu is a receptionist at Electronic Toys.

    She should take Office Machines Training and Being a Team Member.

2. Ed has already had team member training. He's never used the fax machine, though. This week, Ed has some extra time.

    He should take Office Machines Training.

SKILL 4   DEVELOP A PLAN FOR SOLVING A PROBLEM

Imagine that your supervisor says your coworkers aren't working efficiently. Work with a partner or your teacher to develop a plan for solving this problem at your workplace or school.

Performance Review

I can...

☐ 1. understand how my workplace is organized.

☐ 2. identify bosses, coworkers, and direct reports.

☐ 3. identify training needs.

☐ 4. develop a plan for solving a problem.

DISCUSSION

Work with a team. How will the skills help you? Make a list. Share the list with your class.

PRESENTATION

Follow the instructions on page 73.

INFORMAL WORKPLACE-SPECIFIC ASSESSMENT

Ask learners to describe the reporting structure of their job. Who do they directly report to? Does anyone directly report to them? If they have a plan to solve a problem at work, who should they tell?

WORKBOOK

Unit 6, Exercise 9

Talk About It — Adjusting a budget

The Men's Store
Flier Budget for Sweater Sale

Number of Customers	Cost to Print Flier	Cost for Envelopes	Cost for Postage	Cost for Address Labels	Total
2000	(2000 x 6¢) $120	(2000 x 3¢) $60	(2000 x 33¢) $660	(2000 x 1¢) $20	$860

PRACTICE THE DIALOG

A Do you have the budget ready for this month's sale flier?

B Yes, the total cost will be $860.

A That's a little too much money. We have only $800 for advertising this month.

B Well, we can fold and staple the fliers. That way we don't need envelopes. That reduces the cost by $60.

A Good idea.

PARTNER WORK

The store only has $600 to spend on the sale fliers. How can you adjust the budget? Circle the numbers.

1. Send postcards. *(circled)*
2. Use expensive paper.
3. Send fewer fliers. *(circled)*
4. Send more fliers.
5. Use cheaper paper. *(circled)*
6. Use a cheaper printing company. *(circled)*

Talk over ways to adjust the budget. Follow the dialog above.

ASAP PROJECT

Your team has $1,000 to improve your workplace or school. First decide on a project, such as improving the break room or starting a child care room. Then create a budget for the project. Complete this project as you work through the unit.

Unit 7

77

ASAP PROJECT

Have learners read the instructions. Discuss the project and its purpose with learners. Make sure that everyone understands. Help learners assign themselves to teams based upon their knowledge, skills, interests, or other individual strengths. Have each team select a leader. Throughout the rest of the unit, allow time for learners to work on the project. Have the teams agree on a deadline when the project will be finished. For more information, see "ASAP Project" on page vi.

Culture Note

Explain to learners that many companies have an accounting department. The accountants' duties include writing and depositing checks, tracking income and expenses, and making reports.

PREPARATION

1. Display a flier from a local business. Identify the **paper, postage, envelope,** and **label.** Ask learners if their companies use fliers and why they use them.

2. Use prices in a catalog to present or review **expensive** and **cheap.** Explain that a printing company makes books, pamphlets, and other similar products.

PRESENTATION

1. Have learners read and discuss the Purpose Statement. For more information, see "Purpose Statement" on page viii.

2. Focus attention on the budget. Encourage learners to say as much as they can about it. Help them understand each budget category. Write learners' ideas on the board and/or restate them in acceptable English. Then present the dialog. See "Presenting a Dialog" on page ix.

3. Have partners read the Partner Work instructions. Make sure everyone knows what to do. Then have learners complete the activity. Have learners switch partners and repeat. Then have a few pairs present their dialogs to the class.

FOLLOW-UP

Spread the Word: Ask partners to discuss the expenses involved in producing a flier to advertise the class. What could they do to keep the costs as low as possible? For example, would it cost less to mail the flier or post it throughout the community? Which would be the most effective? Have several pairs share their ideas with the class.

♦ Have learners work in teams. Ask team members to imagine that their employers have asked for suggestions on how to reduce company costs. What would they suggest? Have team reporters summarize the discussions for the class.

WORKBOOK

Unit 7, Exercises 3A–3C

SCANS Note

Discuss reasons companies need to maintain quality when they reduce a cost. Ask what will happen, for instance, if a grocery store replaces thick paper bags with less expensive thin bags that tear easily. Ask learners to share examples of budget decisions at their workplaces that maintained quality while reducing costs.

Personal Dictionary

Have learners add the words in their Personal Dictionary to their *Workforce Writing Dictionary.* See "Workforce Writing Dictionary" on page v.

Keep Talking — Prioritizing items on a budget

PRACTICE THE DIALOG

A I think it would be a good idea to get a cooler. We could sell a lot of cold sodas. It may be very good for business.

B Well, we've got $2,000 to spend on equipment. Will that be enough?

B Yes, but we need ten cases of plates and five cases of water glasses.

A OK, that's $750. We have $1,250 left in our equipment budget. Can we buy a cooler for that?

B No, the cheapest two-door cooler's $1,800. With the dishes and glasses, that's $550 more than we have in the budget.

A What if we only buy one case of glasses and three cases of plates now? That would leave enough money in the budget for the cooler. We can get more dishes later.

Stove
$1,300

Cooler
$1,800

Refrigerator
$2,500

Glasses
$50 per case of 36

Plates
$50 per case of 12

PARTNER WORK

The restaurant where you work needs new plates and glasses. You have $500 to spend. Your boss told you to buy six cases of plates and six cases of glasses. Do you have enough money? If not, what do you do? Use the dialog above.

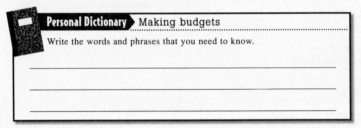

Personal Dictionary ▶ Making budgets

Write the words and phrases that you need to know.

_____

_____

_____

78   Unit 7

PREPARATION

1. Use realia, picture cards, or the restaurant supply catalogs to present **equipment** and **case.**

 2. To present or review **prioritizing,** list school supplies on the board. Have learners arrange the items on the list from most to least important. Identify this process as prioritizing. Discuss why prioritizing is important when making purchases for a business.

PRESENTATION

1. Have learners read the Purpose Statement. See "Purpose Statement" on page viii.

2. Focus attention on the illustrations. Have learners talk about the items and prices. Write their ideas on the board and/or restate them in acceptable English. Then present the dialog. See "Presenting a Dialog" on page ix.

4. Have partners read the Partner Work instructions. Model if necessary. Then have pairs complete the activity. Have learners switch partners and repeat the activity. Have one or two pairs present their dialogs to the class.

5. Have learners read the Personal Dictionary instructions. Then use the Personal Dictionary procedures on page ix. Remind learners to continue to add words to their dictionaries throughout the unit.

FOLLOW-UP

Keeping a Budget: Provide an equipment and supply catalog to each team. Tell teams they have $3,000 for equipment and supplies to set up a small food stand or another small business relevant to learners' jobs or career interests. Ask teams to list their purchases and explain why each is necessary. Have teams compare expense lists.

♦ Tell teams their budget has been reduced from $3,000 to $2,500. Ask them to prepare new expense lists that cut costs. Have team reporters present the new lists and explain how their teams decided which expenses to reduce.

WORKBOOK

Unit 7, Exercise 4

Listening — Using resources wisely

LISTEN AND MATCH

What are they worried about?

Conversation 1 __b__   **a.** display space

Conversation 2 __a__   **b.** budget

Conversation 3 __c__   **c.** new equipment

LISTEN AGAIN

How do they solve the problem? Circle the letter.

1. **a.** save money by finding a cheaper location

   (b.) save money by working as manager

2. **(a.)** put out more regular cola

   b. put out more diet cola

3. **a.** save money by repairing old lawn mowers

   (b.) buy new lawn mowers and leaf-blowers

LISTEN AND CIRCLE

How are the budget expenses prioritized? Circle the letter.

1. Most of the money in the budget should be spent on _____.

   (a.) the trainer   **b.** the inventory control system

2. The least important expense item is _____.

   a. materials   **(b.)** refreshments

3. After the instructor is paid for, the training manuals are _____.

   a. low priority   **(b.)** high priority

Unit 7   79

PREPARATION

1. Use picture cards to present or review **lawn mower** and **leaf-blower.**

2. To present or review **prioritize,** follow the instructions in preparation on page 78.

PRESENTATION

1. Have learners read and discuss the Purpose Statement. For more information, see "Purpose Statement" on page viii.

 2. Have learners read the Listen and Match instructions. Make sure everyone knows what to do. If necessary, model the first item. Then play the tape or read the Listening Transcript aloud two or more times as learners complete the activity. Have learners check their work. See "Presenting a Listening Activity" on page ix.

 3. Have learners read the Listen Again instructions. Then follow the procedures in 2.

 4. Have learners read the Listen and Circle instructions. Then follow the procedures in 2.

FOLLOW-UP

Wise Use of Resources: Have learners work in pairs or small groups to brainstorm a list of expenses at the company they work for (or a company they know about). Ask them to underline the two items on the list they think the company should spend its resources on first. Ask them to circle two items that are low priority. Have a few learners share their ideas with the class.

♦ Ask learners to prioritize their lists, writing the items in order from most to least important. Ask a few learners to read their lists to the class.

WORKBOOK

Unit 7, Exercise 5

Unit 7   79

Grammar ···· Learning the language you need

A. Study the Examples

| The painter | must | estimate how much a job is going to cost. |
| | | cover the furniture carefully. |

| The painter | may | ask for more time to finish a difficult job. |
| | | buy the paint at Pace Hardware Store or Z Mart. |

COMPLETE THE SENTENCES

Circle *may* or *must*.

1. You **may** / **(must)** buy paint before beginning a painting job.
2. The painter **may** / **(must)** cover the carpet.
3. I'm not sure if I'll finish the job today. I **(may)** / **must** take another day to finish it.
4. You **(may)** / **must** paint the rooms in any order you choose. Since no one lives in the house, you can start in any room you want.
5. If you use a ladder, you **may** / **(must)** make sure it's strong.
6. The painter **(may)** / **must** come today or tomorrow. It doesn't matter.

B. Study the Examples

| If you're lucky, you could finish early. |
| You could finish early if you're lucky. |

80

Unit 7

PREPARATION

Review the language in the grammar boxes with learners before they open their books, if necessary.

PRESENTATION

1. Have learners read and discuss the Purpose Statement. For more information, see "Purpose Statement" on page viii.

2. Have learners read the grammar boxes in A. Have learners use the language in the boxes to say as many sentences as possible. Tell learners that they can use the grammar boxes throughout the unit to review or check sentence structures.

3. Focus attention on the photograph. Have learners say as much as they can about it. Encourage learners to use **must** and **may** as they talk about the photo. Write learners' ideas on the board and/or restate them in acceptable English.

4. Focus attention on Complete the Sentences. Make sure that everyone knows what to do. If necessary, model the first item on the board. Then have learners complete the activity independently. Have a different learner read each sentence aloud while the rest of the class checks their answers.

5. Focus attention on the grammar box in B. Follow the procedures in 2.

What could happen? Write a sentence. Use the language in B.

1. The mover's estimate for a moving job is low.

   If the estimate for a moving job is low, the mover could lose money.

2. The painters need light grey paint. The store is out of light grey paint.

   Answers will vary.

   _____

3. The carpenter forgot his hammer at home.

   _____

   _____

4. Mohamed just delivered some bread. The delivery van won't start.

   _____

   _____

5. Diane wants to dry some clothes. The dryer won't heat up.

   _____

   _____

C. Study the Example

Buying products on sale is a good way to save money.

Use the language in C.

1. _____Wearing_____ (**Wear**) a hat keeps paint from getting in your hair.

2. _____Putting_____ (**Put**) a lid on the paint can keeps the paint from drying out.

3. _____Budgeting_____ (**Budget**) the time it takes to do a job is important.

4. _____Cleaning_____ (**Clean**) paintbrushes keeps them from getting stiff.

5. _____Covering_____ (**Cover**) the carpet keeps paint from dripping on it.

6. _____Using_____ (**Use**) a paint roller is faster than using a brush.

Unit 7   81

---

6. Have learners read the instructions for Write. If necessary, model the first item. Then have learners complete the activity independently. Have learners check each other's work in pairs. Ask several learners to read their answers aloud while the rest of the class checks their work.

7. Focus attention on the grammar box in C. Follow the procedures in 2.

8. Focus attention on Complete the Sentences. Then follow the procedures in 4.

FOLLOW-UP

Inventing Sentences: Have learners work in pairs to create **"If..."** sentences like those in B. Have one partner say an **If**-clause, and have the other learner complete the sentence. Ask partners to switch roles and repeat the activity several times. Ask a few pairs to share their sentences with the class.

♦ Have pairs write their sentences. Check learners' work.

WORKBOOK

Unit 7, Exercises 6A–6C

BLACKLINE MASTERS

Blackline Master: Unit 7

Reading and Writing
Evaluating and creating budgets

READ THE BUDGET

TOY ANIMAL MANUFACTURING COSTS
Red Robin Toy Co.

Type of Toy	Labor	Materials	Total Cost per Item
Elephant	$6.00	$4.00	$10.00
Bear	$7.00	$2.00	$9.00
Rabbit	$6.00	$2.00	$8.00
Mouse	$3.00	$1.00	$4.00

READ THE BUDGET

Write *yes* or *no* next to each statement.

_no_ 1. Stores probably charge a high price for a toy mouse.

yes 2. It takes the longest time to make a toy bear.

yes 3. The toy elephant is the most expensive to make.

_no_ 4. The toy bear requires the most materials.

_no_ 5. The toy mouse costs a lot to make because the materials are expensive.

Discussion

What other costs do you think the Red Robin Toy Company has? Make a list.

_____

_____

_____

_____

82

Unit 7

SCANS Note

Explain that the price of an item is higher than the cost because companies need to make a profit. A profit is the difference between the cost and the price. Ask learners what they think would happen if companies did not make a profit.

PREPARATION

Use an item of clothing, a toy, or another product to discuss the difference between the **cost** of manufacturing a product and its sale **price.** Display the product, and ask learners to identify the costs of manufacturing it, such as the materials, labor, packaging, and distribution. Explain that the price a shopper pays for the item is usually higher than total costs.

PRESENTATION

1. Have learners read and discuss the Purpose Statement. For more information, see "Purpose Statement" on page viii.

2. Have learners look over the chart of manufacturing costs. Encourage learners to say everything they can about the chart. Write their ideas on the board and/or restate them in acceptable English.

3. Have learners read the instructions for Read the Budget. Make sure everyone knows what to do. Model the first item if necessary. Then have learners complete the activity independently. Ask several learners to share their answers with the class while the rest of the class checks their work.

4. Have learners read the Discussion question. Then have learners work in teams to list their ideas. Have team reporters share their teams' lists with the class.

READ AND WRITE

Your company needs supplies. Your boss asked you to figure out the cost of the supplies. Fill in the budget. Use the list and the catalog page.

12 rolls of paper towels
2 coffeepots
2 bottles of dishwashing soap
1 box of tea bags

Cross Office Supplies

Call 1-800-555-1213 to order

Break Room Supplies

Paper Towels
$.50 per roll

Deluxe Coffeepots
$3.50 each

Mountain Coffee
$5.00 per bag

Sparkle Dishwashing Soap
$2.00 per bottle

Old English Tea
$6.00 per box of 100 tea bags

Royal Sugar Packets
$6.00 per box of 1000

Supply Budget

Quantity	Item Name	Price Each	Total
12 rolls	paper towels	$.50	$6.00
2	coffeepots	$3.50	$7.00
2 bottles	dishwashing soap	$2.00	$4.00
1 box	tea bags	$6.00	$6.00
		Total	$23.00

DISCUSSION

You showed the budget to your boss. He said he has only $18 to spend. What do you do?

Unit 7

83

---

5. Have learners look over the list of supplies, the catalog page, and the blank budget form. Follow the procedures in 2.

6. Have partners read the Read and Write instructions. Make sure everyone understands what to do. Model if necessary. Then have learners complete the activity independently. Have several different learners each read a line of their completed supply budgets while the rest of the class checks their answers.

7. Have learners read the Discussion question. Then have learners work in teams to discuss their ideas. Have team reporters share their teams' ideas with the class.

FOLLOW-UP

Adjust a Budget: Have teams discuss other ways they could use the $18 to purchase supplies. Have them make a list of questions they might ask their coworkers to help them prioritize purchases for the break room. Have team reporters share the list of questions with the class.

♦ Ask partners to practice telling a supervisor that there isn't enough money in the budget for break room supplies. One partner should role-play the employee; the other, the boss. Ask partners to switch roles and repeat. Have several partners present their dialogs to the class.

WORKBOOK

Unit 7, Exercises 7A–7B

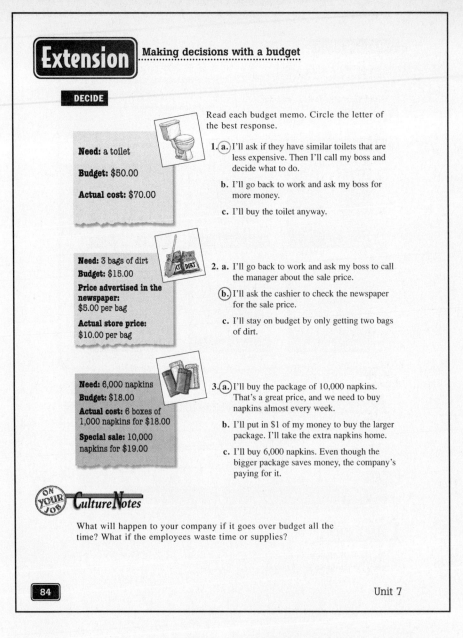

Extension ········ Making decisions with a budget ········

DECIDE

Read each budget memo. Circle the letter of the best response.

Need: a toilet

Budget: $50.00

Actual cost: $70.00

1. (a.) I'll ask if they have similar toilets that are less expensive. Then I'll call my boss and decide what to do.

   b. I'll go back to work and ask my boss for more money.

   c. I'll buy the toilet anyway.

Need: 3 bags of dirt
Budget: $15.00
Price advertised in the newspaper: $5.00 per bag
Actual store price: $10.00 per bag

2. a. I'll go back to work and ask my boss to call the manager about the sale price.

   (b.) I'll ask the cashier to check the newspaper for the sale price.

   c. I'll stay on budget by only getting two bags of dirt.

Need: 6,000 napkins
Budget: $18.00
Actual cost: 6 boxes of 1,000 napkins for $18.00
Special sale: 10,000 napkins for $19.00

3. (a.) I'll buy the package of 10,000 napkins. That's a great price, and we need to buy napkins almost every week.

   b. I'll put in $1 of my money to buy the larger package. I'll take the extra napkins home.

   c. I'll buy 6,000 napkins. Even though the bigger package saves money, the company's paying for it.

Culture Notes

What will happen to your company if it goes over budget all the time? What if the employees waste time or supplies?

84 Unit 7

PREPARATION

Use newspaper advertising inserts as you talk about the difference in price between a single can of soda and a six-pack. Ask learners when it makes sense to buy the single can and when they might buy the six-pack.

PRESENTATION

1. Have learners read and discuss the Purpose Statement. See "Purpose Statement" on page viii.

2. Have learners preview the budget memos and look at the illustrations. Encourage them to say everything they can about them. Write their ideas on the board and/or restate them in acceptable English. Then have learners read the budget memos independently.

3. Have partners read the instructions for Decide. Make sure everyone knows what to do. If necessary, model the first item. Then have learners complete the activity. Ask several learners to share their responses while the rest of the class checks their work.

 4. Have learners read Culture Notes and talk over their responses in teams. Have team reporters share their teams' ideas with the class. Ask the teams to compare each other's ideas. See "Culture Notes" on page vii.

FOLLOW-UP

Decisions: Give each team a newspaper advertising insert and a budget memo that lists a few items advertised in the insert. Specify the quantities they need to buy and the total amount they may spend. Make sure at least one team will

be on budget, under budget, and over budget. Have teams find the items in the ad, calculate total spending, and decide what to do. Have teams share their ideas with the class.

♦ Ask teams to brainstorm ideas for finding the best deals when they shop. Have team reporters share their teams' ideas with the class.

WORKBOOK

Unit 7, Exercise 8

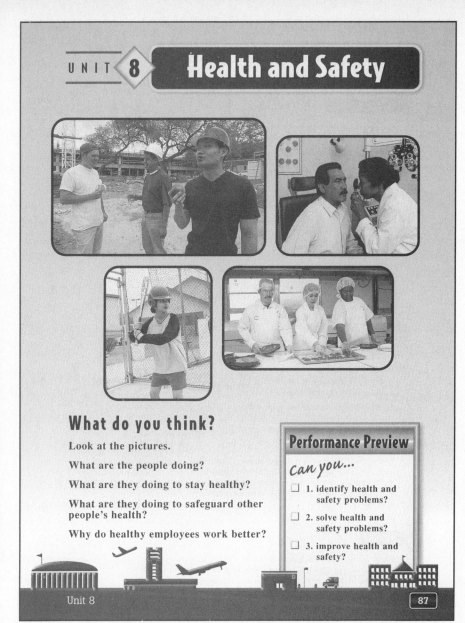

UNIT 8 — Health and Safety

What do you think?

Look at the pictures.

What are the people doing?

What are they doing to stay healthy?

What are they doing to safeguard other people's health?

Why do healthy employees work better?

Performance Preview

can you...

☐ 1. identify health and safety problems?

☐ 2. solve health and safety problems?

☐ 3. improve health and safety?

Unit 8

87

Unit 8 Overview
—SCANS Competencies—

★ Monitor and correct performance

★ Select equipment and tools

★ Interpret information

Workforce Skills

- Identify health and safety problems
- Solve health and safety problems
- Improve health and safety

Materials

- Picture cards or realia of unsafe and safe work situations, the human spine, the food pyramid, goggles, a questionnaire, hobbies, a skull and crossbones poison symbol
- Two sheets of posterboard
- Books or brochures with pictures of stretching exercises
- Pictures or equipment catalog to show a circular saw, blowtorch, electric drill, and workbench

Unit Warm-Up

To get learners thinking about the unit topic (improving health and safety), act out a safety problem, such as slipping on a wet floor. Have learners talk about ways to solve the problem.

★　　★　　★　　★　　★

WORKFORCE SKILLS (page 87)

Identify health and safety problems

Solve health and safety problems

Improve health and safety

★　　★　　★　　★　　★

PREPARATION

1. Display picture cards of safe and unsafe work situations. Ask learners to sort the cards and explain what's wrong in the unsafe situations.

2. Ask learners to talk about how an employee's health may affect customers, coworkers, and the employee's work performance. Ask: *What may happen if people go to work when they're sick?*

PRESENTATION

1. Focus attention on the photographs. Ask learners what they think the unit might be about. Write their ideas on the board and/or restate them in acceptable English.

2. Have learners talk about the photographs. Ask learners to describe the situations and identify the health and/or safety practices in each. Help learners identify special clothing or safety equipment.

3. Help learners read the questions. Discuss the questions with the class.

4. You may want to use the Performance Preview to provide learners with an overview of the skills in the unit. Have learners read the list of skills and discuss what they will learn in the unit.

FOLLOW-UP

Brainstorming: Have teams brainstorm a list of things team members do to maintain their health and stay safe, such as wearing seat belts, getting enough sleep, and eating healthfully. Have team reporters write the lists on the board.

♦ Help the class create a master list of all the ways learners maintain their health and safety. Post the list in the classroom.

WORKBOOK

Unit 8, Exercises 1A–1B

Getting Started · Identifying health and safety problems

PARTNER WORK

The people in the mail room have had some problems lately. Look at the picture and say what's wrong.

TEAM WORK

Match the advice with the people.

a. She should sit up in her chair.
b. He should have a better diet.
c. He should lift correctly.
d. She should clean up her work area.

PARTNER WORK

You work at the company in the picture. The boss wants your recommendations on how to improve the workplace. Write your recommendations in order of importance. Share your recommendations with the class.

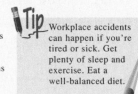
Tip Workplace accidents can happen if you're tired or sick. Get plenty of sleep and exercise. Eat a well-balanced diet.

SURVEY

Work with a team. Each person names a workplace safety issue that they worry about. Have the team think of a solution for each problem. Make a chart of problems and solutions.

88   Unit 8

Teaching Note

Use this page to introduce the new language in the unit. Whenever possible, encourage peer teaching. Supply any language learners need.

SCANS Note

Make learners aware that a safety procedure completed by one worker can ensure the safety of many other people. A worker who quickly cleans up a spilled liquid, for instance, spares coworkers and customers possible injuries.

PREPARATION

Use pantomime to present or review **sit up** and **lift**. Explain that what a person eats is his or her **diet**.

PRESENTATION

1. Have learners read and discuss the Purpose Statement. See "Purpose Statement" on page viii.

2. Focus attention on the illustration. Encourage learners to say everything they can about it. Write learners' ideas on the board and/or restate them in acceptable English.

3. Have learners read the Partner Work instructions. Make sure everyone knows what to do. Have pairs complete the activity. Ask one or two pairs to share their answers with the class.

4. Have teams read the Team Work instructions. Make sure each team knows what to do. If necessary, model the first item. Then have teams complete the activity. Have team reporters share the answers with the class.

5. Have partners read the Partner Work instructions. Follow the procedures in 3.

 6. Have learners read the Survey instructions. Make sure everyone knows what to do. Then have teams complete the activity. Have teams compare their charts.

Tip Have learners read the Tip independently, then discuss how the advice will help them. See "Presenting a Tip" on page ix."

FOLLOW-UP

Bar Graphs: Have teams create tables showing the average number of hours per night each learner sleeps. Then have teams show the information on bar graphs, with hours of sleep on the vertical axis and the number of learners' names on the horizontal axis. Display graphs in the classroom.

♦ Ask teams to discuss the effects of not getting enough sleep. How could lack of sleep affect work? How could it affect safety? Ask team reporters to share their teams' ideas with the class.

WORKBOOK

Unit 8, Exercises 2A–2B

 **Talk About It** .... Solving workstation problems

TEAM WORK

What's wrong with his workstation? Talk about it. Tell the class.

 PRACTICE THE DIALOG

A Can you help me? My back hurts all the time. Do you think it could be my chair?

B Maybe. Does it always lean backwards like this?

A I think so. Do you know how to fix it?

B Let me show you. You might want to raise it, too. It looks a little low.

 PARTNER WORK

Talk about ways employees can injure themselves at your workplace or a workplace you know. Say what you think they should do to prevent these injuries. Then create a dialog in which you give safety advice to an employee. Follow the dialog above.

> **Useful language**
>
> Stand up and stretch every hour.
>
> Wear a back-support belt.

ASAP
PROJECT

Work in two teams. One team makes a poster of ways to promote health at work. The other team creates a poster about ways to increase workplace safety. Present your posters to the class. Complete this project as you work through the unit.

Unit 8   89

ASAP
PROJECT

Have learners read the instructions. Discuss the project and its purpose with learners. Make sure that everyone understands. Give each team a sheet of posterboard. Help learners assign themselves to teams based upon their knowledge, skills, interests, or other individual strengths. Have each team select a leader. Throughout the rest of the unit, allow time for learners to work on the project. Have the teams agree on a deadline when the posters will be finished. For more information, see "ASAP Project" on page vi.

Culture Note

Suggest that learners evaluate their workstations for health or safety problems. Explain that many workstation problems are easily solved by raising or lowering chairs, work surfaces, and/or equipment. Ask learners to describe changes in workstations that might improve health and safety.

PREPARATION

1. Clarify the new language on the page by leaning **backward** in a chair. Use role-play as you explain that your back **hurts.**

2. Ask learners to talk about health or safety issues that are associated with the equipment they use at work.

PRESENTATION

1. Have learners read and discuss the Purpose Statement. See "Purpose Statement" on page viii.

2. Focus attention on the photograph. Have learners say as much as they can about it. Write their ideas on the board and/or restate them in acceptable English.

3. Have teams read the Team Work instructions. Make sure each team knows what to do. Then have teams complete the activity. Have team reporters summarize the discussions for the class. Then present the dialog. See "Presenting a Dialog" on page ix.

 4. Have partners read the Partner Work instructions. Then focus attention on the Useful Language box. Help learners read the expressions. If necessary, model pronunciation. Then have learners complete the activity. Have learners switch partners and repeat several times. Have one or two pairs present their dialogs to the class.

FOLLOW-UP

Stretch and Tone: Provide books or pamphlets with pictures of stretching exercises designed for workplace situations and appropriate to your learners' age and abilities. Assign each team one or two exercises. Have teams practice their exercises and then teach them to the class.

♦ Have teams act out unhealthy workstation habits, such as slouching. Ask other teams to suggest the problems that each unhealthy habit can cause.

WORKBOOK

Unit 8, Exercises 3A–3B

WORKFORCE SKILLS (page 90)

Identify health and safety problems

Improve health and safety

★ ★ ★ ★ ★

SCANS Note

Tell learners that sore backs are the number one reason employees miss work. Explain that employees can avoid many back injuries if they follow safety instructions and use proper safety equipment. Volunteers may wish to share experiences with back injuries.

Personal Dictionary

Have learners add the words in their Personal Dictionary to their *Workforce Writing Dictionary*. For more information, see "Workforce Writing Dictionary" on page v.

Keep Talking ⋯⋯ Being aware of health and safety problems

incorrect   correct

PRACTICE THE DIALOG

A You're not lifting that box right. You could get hurt. Make sure you lift it correctly.

B Can you show me how?

A Sure. Don't bend from the waist. Keep your back straight. Bend your knees. Keep the box close to your body. Then straighten your legs.

B Thanks.

PARTNER WORK

Take turns showing and telling each other how to lift objects correctly. Follow the dialog above.

Personal Dictionary ▸ Solving Health and Safety Problems ⋯

Write the words and phrases that you need to know.

_____

_____

_____

90   Unit 8

PREPARATION

Have learners brainstorm a list of phrases they can use to report unsafe situations at work. Write the list on the board.

PRESENTATION

1. Have learners read the Purpose Statement. For more information, see "Purpose Statement" on page viii.

 2. Focus attention on the photographs. Have learners explain the different methods of lifting. Write their ideas on the board and/or restate them in acceptable English. Then present the dialog. See "Presenting a Dialog" on page ix.

3. Have partners read the Partner Work instructions. Model if necessary. Make

sure everyone knows what to do. Then have learners complete the activity. Have learners switch partners and repeat the activity. Have one or two partners present their dialogs to the class.

4. Have learners read the Personal Dictionary instructions. Then use the Personal Dictionary procedures on page ix. Remind learners to continue to add words to their dictionaries throughout the unit.

FOLLOW-UP

Stand Tall: Display a picture of the human spine. Tell learners that one reason a healthy back is important is that major nerves in the body branch out from the spine. Explain that exercise and good posture help maintain a

healthy back. Separate the class into two teams. Have one team talk about back and stomach exercises that strengthen back muscles. Have the other team discuss good posture and ways to maintain it. Ask team reporters to share ideas with the class.

♦ Have pairs create a list of rules for lifting heavy objects safely. Ask several learners to read their lists to the class.

WORKBOOK

Unit 8, Exercise 4A–4B

Listening — Identifying health and safety resources

LISTEN AND CIRCLE

What is the cause of each health or safety problem? Circle the letter.

1. Diego isn't feeling well because he _____.

   a. smokes   **b.** is overweight

2. Eva feels nervous because she doesn't _____.

   a. exercise   **b.** eat right

3. Lupe has no energy because she needs more _____.

   a. vitamins   **b.** sleep

LISTEN AGAIN

What can help with each employee's problem? Write the letter.

_c_ **1.** Diego   **a.** a class

_a_ **2.** Eva   **b.** help from her husband

_b_ **3.** Lupe   ~~**c.**~~ company

LISTEN AND CIRCLE

1. Why does Paul have headaches?

   a. He's under a lot of stress.   **b.** He drinks a lot of coffee.

2. What has Paul done for his headaches?

   a. He's stayed home.   **b.** He's taken aspirin.

3. Why did Paul stop going to the gym?

   a. He hurt his shoulder.

   b. He didn't like it.

4. What does Paul's coworker recommend?

   a. He thinks Paul should get some exercise.

   b. He thinks Paul should spend time with friends.

5. What do Paul and his coworker decide to do together?

   a. They decide to go to the gym.

   b. They decide to exercise at lunch time.

Unit 8   91

Culture Note

Discuss different resources for information about health and safety issues. Examples include human resources departments, courses at trade and technical schools and at community colleges, and libraries.

PREPARATION

Use pantomime to teach or review **cough, nervous, headache, stress,** and **overweight.** Have learners talk about solutions for these health problems or resources that help people deal with them.

PRESENTATION

1. Have learners read and discuss the Purpose Statement. For more information, see "Purpose Statement" on page viii.

 2. Have learners read the Listen and Circle instructions. Make sure everyone knows what to do. If necessary, model the first item. Then play the tape or read the Listening Transcript aloud two or more times as learners complete the activity.

Have learners check their work. For more information, see "Presenting a Listening Activity" on page ix.

 3. Have learners read the Listen Again instructions. Then follow the procedures in 2.

 4. Have learners read the Listen and Circle instructions. Then follow the procedures in 2.

FOLLOW-UP

Cause, Effect, and Treatment: On separate slips of paper, write health and safety problems, such as "smoking cigarettes," "lifting incorrectly," and "stress." Give each team of three one slip. Have the teams discuss the possible harmful effects and identify a resource or an activity that can help. Have several teams present their ideas to the class.

♦ Have learners work in pairs to create dialogs about a health problem. Have one learner describe the problem; have the other suggest a cause and a solution. Have several pairs present their dialogs to the class.

WORKBOOK

Unit 8, Exercises 5A–5B

Identify health and safety problems

Solve health and safety problems

Improve health and safety

★   ★   ★   ★   ★

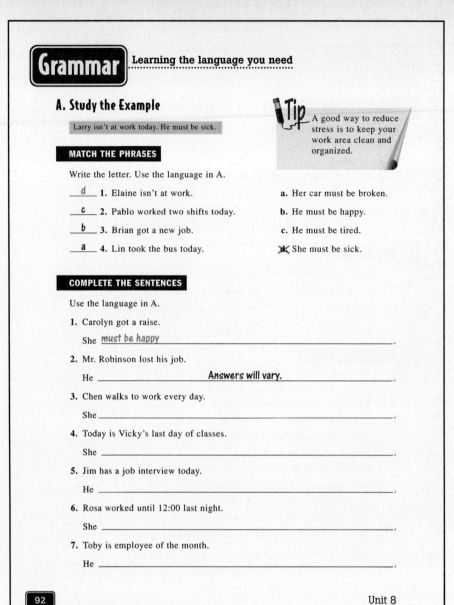

Language Note

*Explain that some verbs have irregular forms in the past tense. Examples on these pages include **get/got**, **take/took**, **lose/lost**. Use the verbs in sample sentences. Encourage learners to use the verbs in their own sentences.*

PREPARATION

Review the language in the grammar boxes with learners before they open their books, if necessary.

PRESENTATION

1. Have learners read and discuss the Purpose Statement. For more information, see "Purpose Statement" on page viii.

2. Have learners read the grammar box in A. Have learners use the language in the box to say as many sentences as possible. Tell learners that they can use the grammar box throughout the unit to review or check sentence structures.

3. Focus attention on Match the Phrases. If necessary, model the first item. Then have learners complete the activity independently. Have a different

learner read each answer aloud while the rest of the class checks their answers.

4. Focus attention on Complete the Sentences. If necessary, model the first item. Then have learners complete the activity independently. Have several learners read a sentence aloud while the rest of the class checks their answers.

Have learners read the Tip independently. Have learners discuss how the advice will help them. For more information, see "Presenting a Tip" on page ix.

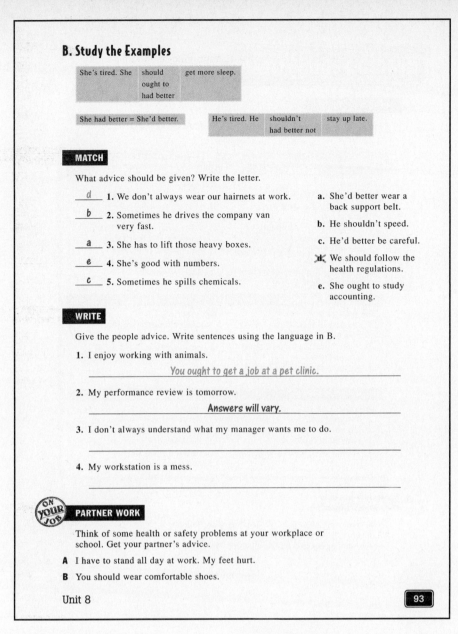

B. Study the Examples

| She's tired. She | should
ought to
had better | get more sleep. |

| She had better = She'd better. | | He's tired. He | shouldn't
had better not | stay up late. |

MATCH

What advice should be given? Write the letter.

___d___ 1. We don't always wear our hairnets at work.

___b___ 2. Sometimes he drives the company van very fast.

___a___ 3. She has to lift those heavy boxes.

___e___ 4. She's good with numbers.

___c___ 5. Sometimes he spills chemicals.

a. She'd better wear a back support belt.

b. He shouldn't speed.

c. He'd better be careful.

d. We should follow the health regulations.

e. She ought to study accounting.

WRITE

Give the people advice. Write sentences using the language in B.

1. I enjoy working with animals.

   _____*You ought to get a job at a pet clinic.*_____

2. My performance review is tomorrow.

   _____**Answers will vary.**_____

3. I don't always understand what my manager wants me to do.

   _____

4. My workstation is a mess.

   _____

PARTNER WORK

Think of some health or safety problems at your workplace or school. Get your partner's advice.

A I have to stand all day at work. My feet hurt.

B You should wear comfortable shoes.

Unit 8   `93`

---

5. Focus attention on the grammar boxes in B. Follow the procedures in 2.

6. Focus attention on Match and follow the procedures in 3.

7. Focus attention on Write. If necessary, model the first item. Then have learners complete the activity independently. Have several learners share their advice for each item while the rest of the class checks their answers.

 8. Have partners read the Partner Work instructions. Make sure everyone understands what to do. Then have learners complete the activity. Have learners switch partners and repeat several times. Have several pairs present their dialogs to the class.

FOLLOW-UP

Good Advice: On blank slips of paper, write descriptions of an employee's problem at work *(He fell asleep; She has a sore back; She can't find anything on her desk)*. Have teams choose a slip and give advice, using the language in the grammar box in B. Ask team reporters to present the problems and their teams' advice.

♦ Have teams write their problem and their advice on a sheet of paper. Then ask teams to exchange papers and suggest additional advice for the same problem. Continue until all teams have given advice on all the problems. Have teams read all the advice to the class.

WORKBOOK

Unit 8, Exercises 6A–6B

BLACKLINE MASTERS

Blackline Master: Unit 8

★   ★   ★   ★   ★

Language Note

*Explain that some verbs change meaning when used with the word **up**. Examples on these pages include **get up**, **sit up**, and **warm up**. Use these phrases in sample sentences, and ask learners to compare the meaning of the phrases to the meaning of the verbs alone. Brainstorm with learners a list of other verbs that change meaning with **up**, such as **catch up**, **make up**, **pick up**, **give up**, **bring up**, **look up**, and **turn up**.*

Reading and Writing — Improving health and safety

READ AND ANSWER

Read the questionnaire. Check the boxes of the things you do.

Employee Wellness QUESTIONNAIRE

Diet

Do you . . .
- ❑ avoid fatty foods?
- ❑ eat vegetables and fruits every day?
- ❑ eat five or more servings of grains each day?
- ❑ eat at least one well-balanced meal every day?
- ❑ drink eight glasses of water or juice daily?

Workplace Safety

Do you . . .
- ❑ vary motions at work?
- ❑ stretch at work?
- ❑ sit up straight at work?
- ❑ wear a back-support brace, goggles, or other safety equipment as needed?
- ❑ get regular medical, dental, and eye exams?

Exercise

Do you . . .
- ❑ exercise at least three times a week?
- ❑ stretch and warm up before you exercise?
- ❑ exercise the muscles you use at work?

Sleep

Do you . . .
- ❑ sleep at least six to eight hours each night?
- ❑ go to sleep and get up at about the same times every day?

Stress

Do you . . .
- ❑ like your job?
- ❑ like your coworkers?
- ❑ have hobbies?
- ❑ enjoy your friends and family?

Addictions

Do you . . .
- ❑ drink less than two glasses of alcohol each day?
- ❑ drink less than two drinks with caffeine every day?
- ❑ avoid smoking?

PARTNER WORK

Think over your answers to the questionnaire. Talk about your good habits. How do they help you at your workplace or school? Do you want to develop any new habits? Which ones? Why?

94

Unit 8

PREPARATION

1. Use a picture card of the food pyramid to clarify **servings, grains,** and **well-balanced.**

2. Use realia, picture cards, or pantomime to present or review **questionnaire, muscles, hobbies,** and **goggles.**

3. Use pantomime to demonstrate the meaning of the phrase **vary motions.**

PRESENTATION

1. Have learners read and discuss the Purpose Statement. For more information, see "Purpose Statement" on page viii.

2. Have learners preview the questionnaire before they answer it. See "Prereading" on page x. Encourage learners to say everything they can about it. Write their ideas on the board and/or restate them in acceptable English.

3. Have learners read the instructions for Read and Answer. Make sure everyone knows what to do. Model an item if necessary. Then have learners complete the activity independently. Allow learners to keep the results of the questionnaire private if they wish.

 4. Have partners read the Partner Work instructions. Make sure everyone understands what to do. Then have learners complete the activity. Have learners switch partners and repeat several times. Have one or two partners present their dialogs to the class.

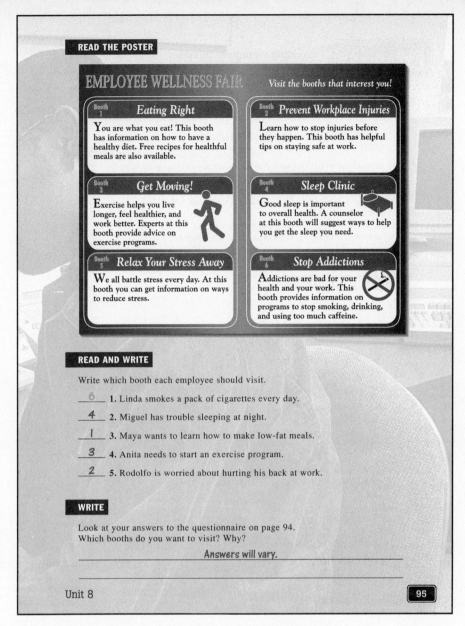

EMPLOYEE WELLNESS FAIR

Visit the booths that interest you!

Booth 1 — Eating Right

You are what you eat! This booth has information on how to have a healthy diet. Free recipes for healthful meals are also available.

Booth 2 — Prevent Workplace Injuries

Learn how to stop injuries before they happen. This booth has helpful tips on staying safe at work.

Booth 3 — Get Moving!

Exercise helps you live longer, feel healthier, and work better. Experts at this booth provide advice on exercise programs.

Booth 4 — Sleep Clinic

Good sleep is important to overall health. A counselor at this booth will suggest ways to help you get the sleep you need.

Booth 5 — Relax Your Stress Away

We all battle stress every day. At this booth you can get information on ways to reduce stress.

Booth 6 — Stop Addictions

Addictions are bad for your health and your work. This booth provides information on programs to stop smoking, drinking, and using too much caffeine.

READ AND WRITE

Write which booth each employee should visit.

_6_ 1. Linda smokes a pack of cigarettes every day.

_4_ 2. Miguel has trouble sleeping at night.

_1_ 3. Maya wants to learn how to make low-fat meals.

_3_ 4. Anita needs to start an exercise program.

_2_ 5. Rodolfo is worried about hurting his back at work.

WRITE

Look at your answers to the questionnaire on page 94. Which booths do you want to visit? Why?

Answers will vary.

_____

Unit 8   **95**

Culture Note

Explain that "wellness" includes taking steps to keep from getting sick, an approach to health known as "preventative medicine." Have learners talk about ways they practice preventative medicine, such as getting enough sleep or exercising regularly.

5. Have learners preview the poster. Follow the procedures in 2.

6. Have partners read the instructions for Read and Write. Make sure everyone understands what to do. Model if necessary. Then have learners complete the activity independently. Have several learners read their responses while the rest of the class checks their answers.

7. Have learners read the Write instructions. Make sure everyone knows what to do. Model the activity if necessary. Then have learners complete the activity. Have several learners share their answers with the class.

FOLLOW-UP

Wellness Fair: Have learners work in pairs. Ask them to choose one of the booths at the Wellness Fair and create a dialog between a worker and an expert at the booth. Have several pairs present their dialogs to the class.

♦ Have learners switch roles and "go to another booth at the Wellness Fair." Have them create new dialogs. Ask them to continue to visit booths and switch roles until they've visited every booth at the Fair. Have several pairs present their dialogs to the class.

WORKBOOK

Unit 8, Exercises 7A–7C

Solve health and safety problems

Improve health and safety

★　　★　　★　　★　　★

Language Note

Tell learners that every profession has special vocabulary to describe its tools and activities. A carpenter, for example, uses a workbench, and a welder uses a blow torch. Ask learners for examples of special terms used in their workplaces.

 **Extension** ···· Preventing workplace injuries ····

 READ THE TIPS

R Reliable Homebuilders

Tips for Preventing Workplace Injuries

It's your job to help prevent injuries. Please follow these guidelines.

1. Take short breaks between repeated motions. Stretch at least once an hour.
2. Wear all your safety gear.
3. Use caution with sharp tools and machines. Make sure all safety guards are operating properly.
4. Ask for help or use equipment for heavy lifting.
5. Adjust the height and placement of chairs, keyboards, and equipment.

 **WHAT SHOULD THEY DO?**

Write the tip number on the line.

__1__ 1. Sara uses an electric drill all day.

__5__ 2. Eduardo's workbench is too high.

__4__ 3. Al can't lift some heavy boxes.

__2__ 4. Anita is using the blowtorch, and she's not wearing her safety goggles.

__3__ 5. Fu is using a circular saw.

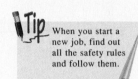 **Tip** When you start a new job, find out all the safety rules and follow them.

 Discussion

Do any of the rules apply to jobs at your workplace? Which ones? Does your workplace have other safety rules like these? Share your ideas with the class.

Culture Notes

If you become sick or injured at work, you need to report it right away. Why do you think this is necessary? What should you say? Who should you tell?

96   Unit 8

PREPARATION

Use picture cards or pictures from an equipment catalog to teach or review **electric drill, workbench, blow torch,** and **circular saw.**

PRESENTATION

1. Have learners read and discuss the Purpose Statement. See "Purpose Statement" on page viii.

2. Have learners preview the tips before they read. Encourage them to say everything they can about them. Supply any language needed. Then have learners read the tips independently.

3. Have partners read the instructions under What Should They Do? Make sure everyone knows what to do. Then have learners complete the activity independently. Have several learners share their responses while the rest of the class checks their answers.

 4. Have learners read the Discussion questions. Then have them work in teams to discuss their ideas. Have team reporters share the ideas with the class.

 5. Have learners read Culture Notes and talk over their responses in teams. Have team reporters share the ideas with the class.

Tip Have learners read the Tip independently, then talk about safety rules where they work. See "Presenting a Tip" on page ix.

FOLLOW-UP

Stop and Go: Have learners work in teams. Have each team write a description of a safe or unsafe workplace situation. As the team reads its description aloud, other teams should say "Stop!" if the situation is unsafe and "Go!" if it is safe. If unsafe, have learners suggest corrections.

♦ Display the skull and crossbones symbol. Discuss its meaning. Ask teams to describe other safety symbols they have seen. As a class, discuss how symbols can help warn people about danger.

WORKBOOK

Unit 8, Exercise 8

Performance Check

How well can you use the skills in this unit?

Complete the activities. Go over your work with a partner or your teacher. Then complete the Performance Review on page 98.

SKILL 1 **IDENTIFY HEALTH AND SAFETY PROBLEMS**

Look at the pictures. What are the health or safety problems in the situations? Tell a partner or your teacher.

SKILL 2 **SOLVE HEALTH AND SAFETY PROBLEMS**

What's wrong with Marge's workstation? Tell your partner or your teacher what Marge should do differently.

Unit 8

97

PRESENTATION

Use any of the procedures in "Evaluation," page x, with pages 97 and 98. Record individuals' results on the Unit 8 Individual Competency Chart. Record the class's results on the Class Cumulative Competency Chart.

Write the number of the booth each employee should visit.

Company Wellness Fair   *Visit the booths that interest you!*

BOOTH 1 • Sleep Clinic

Good sleep is important to overall health. A counselor at this booth will suggest ways to get the sleep you need. She will analyze your sleep patterns and make suggestions.

BOOTH 2 • Stop Addictions

Smoking, excessive drinking, and illegal drugs are bad for your health. This booth provides information on programs to help people overcome these problems.

BOOTH 3 • Eating Right

You are what you eat! This booth has information on how to have a healthy diet. Free recipes for low-fat meals will be available.

BOOTH 4 • Get Moving!

Exercise helps you live longer, feel healthier, and work better. Experts at this booth provide advice on exercise programs.

_3_ 1. Tim wants to learn to cook low-fat meals.

_1_ 2. Wanda can't fall asleep before 3:00 in the morning, no matter how tired she is.

_4_ 3. Chen can't run anymore because of an injury. She wants to find another type of exercise she likes to do.

Performance Review

I can...

☐ 1. identify health and safety problems.

☐ 2. solve health and safety problems.

☐ 3. improve health and safety.

DISCUSSION

Work with a team. How will the skills help you? Make a list. Share the list with your class.

Unit 8

PRESENTATION

Follow the instructions on page 97.

INFORMAL WORKPLACE-SPECIFIC ASSESSMENT

Ask learners to describe a health or safety problem at their workplace and suggest a solution or a resource to deal with it.

WORKBOOK

Unit 8, Exercise 9

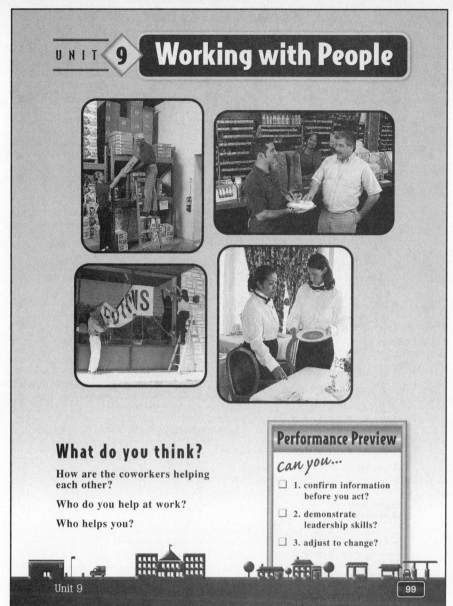

UNIT 9 — Working with People

What do you think?

How are the coworkers helping each other?

Who do you help at work?

Who helps you?

Performance Preview

Can you...

- ☐ 1. confirm information before you act?
- ☐ 2. demonstrate leadership skills?
- ☐ 3. adjust to change?

Unit 9

99

★ Acquire and evaluate data

★ Monitor and correct performance

★ Design or improve systems

★ Lead

Workforce Skills

- Confirm information before you act
- Demonstrate leadership skills
- Adjust to change

Materials

- Picture cards of tasks that require more than one person; a small store, such as a jewelry store; a cab, luggage, guests, and a uniform
- Help wanted pages from newspapers

Unit Warm-Up

To get learners thinking about the unit topic (demonstrating leadership and adjusting to change), ask one or two volunteers to lead the class in a discussion of a current news event, an event at learners' workplaces, or another topic of interest to learners. Ask learners if they would be comfortable in the leader's role. Ask why or why not.

★ ★ ★ ★ ★

WORKFORCE SKILLS (page 99)

Demonstrate leadership skills

★ ★ ★ ★ ★

PREPARATION

Discuss and/or display pictures of tasks that require more than one person, such as caring for a group of toddlers. Ask learners how many people they think should work together to perform each task. Discuss tasks at learners' workplaces that require more than one person.

PRESENTATION

1. Focus attention on the photographs. Ask learners to speculate what the unit might be about. Write their ideas on the board and/or restate them in acceptable English.

2. Have learners talk about the photographs. Help them identify the occupation and describe what's going on in each picture.

3. Help learners read the questions. Discuss the questions with the class.

4. You may want to use the Performance Preview to provide learners with an overview of the skills in the unit. Have learners read the list of skills and discuss what they will learn in the unit.

FOLLOW-UP

Taking the Lead: Divide the class into two teams. Ask one team to assign its members roles as workers in a grocery store, including a shift manager, stock clerks, cashiers, and baggers. Ask the other team to assign roles in a restaurant, including a shift manager, bussers, servers, and a cook. Have teams develop short skits showing the managers guiding the employees as they work. Ask teams to present the skits to the class.

♦ Ask learners to list qualities they admire in leaders they know. List their ideas on the board. Help the class consolidate the information into a "top ten" list of leadership qualities.

WORKBOOK

Unit 9, Exercises 1A–1B

Teaching Note

Use this page to introduce the new language in the unit. Whenever possible, encourage peer teaching. Supply any new language learners need.

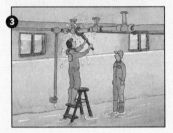

Getting Started — Taking action

TEAM WORK

Look at each picture. What's the problem? Which employee's taking action? What would you do?

PARTNER WORK

Student A talks about a problem. Student B offers a solution.

A A pipe is broken.

B Let's shut off the water.

SURVEY

Work with a team. Think of a problem that can happen at your workplace or school. Then ask other learners for ideas on how to solve the problem. What's the most common solution? What's the most original solution?

100   Unit 9

PREPARATION

Display a picture of a small store, such as a jewelry shop. Tell learners they work the early shift at this store. They arrive at work and find the front window broken. Ask: *What is the problem? What would you do?* Encourage multiple responses.

PRESENTATION

1. Have learners read and discuss the Purpose Statement. See "Purpose Statement" on page viii.

2. Focus attention on the illustrations. Have learners say as much as they can about them. Write their ideas on the board and/or restate them in acceptable English.

3. Have teams read the Team Work instructions. Make sure each team

knows what to do. If necessary, model the first answer. Then have teams complete the activity. Have team reporters share their teams' answers with the class.

4. Have partners read the Partner Work instructions. If necessary, model the activity. Have partners complete the activity, switch partners, and repeat the activity. Ask a few pairs to present their dialogs to the class.

5. Have learners read the Survey instructions. Then have teams complete the activity. Have team reporters share the teams' answers with the class.

FOLLOW-UP

Problem-Solving Tips: On separate slips of paper, write tips that will help

solve problems, such as: *get more information, ask a coworker for help, call a repair person, replace equipment, speak to the manager.* Have each team draw a slip and brainstorm work problems for which that tip would be useful. Have team reporters read the lists to the class.

♦ Write all the tips from the slips of paper on the board. Have the class add other tips for solving problems that have worked for them at their workplaces.

WORKBOOK

Unit 9, Exercises 2A–2B

Talk About It — Checking information

PRACTICE THE DIALOG

A Alice, Mr. Hernandez says that his office isn't very clean. He says the cleaning crew never vacuums or empties the trash.

B Really? I'll check the office. Then I'll talk to the cleaning crew.

DISCUSSION

Why did Alice check the office before speaking with the cleaning crew? What should Alice do if she finds out Mr. Hernandez's office is dirty? What should Alice do if Mr. Hernandez's office is clean?

PARTNER WORK

A waiter complains to the restaurant manager that the cooks take too long to prepare his orders. He says the other waiters get their orders much faster. How does the manager respond? Take turns complaining and responding.

ASAP PROJECT

Work with a team. Create a problem-solving handbook. Each page should contain a common workplace problem and one or two possible solutions. Complete this project as you work through the unit.

Unit 9

101

ASAP PROJECT

Have learners read the instructions. Discuss the project and its purpose with learners. Make sure everyone understands. Help learners assign themselves to teams based upon their knowledge, skills, interests, or other individual strengths. Have each team select a leader, and have the team leaders or the whole class select an overall project leader. Throughout the rest of the unit, allow time for learners to work on the project. Have the teams agree on a deadline when the project will be finished. For more information, see "ASAP Project" on page vi.

PREPARATION

To present or review **complaining** and **responding,** act out a situation in which a restaurant customer tells a manager that the food is cold. Ask which person is complaining and which is responding. Have learners give examples of complaints they have heard at their workplaces.

PRESENTATION

1. Have learners read and discuss the Purpose Statement. See "Purpose Statement" on page viii.

2. Focus attention on the photograph. Encourage learners to say as much as they can about it. Write their ideas on the board and/or restate them in acceptable English. Then present the dialog. See "Presenting a Dialog" on page ix.

3. Have teams read the Discussion instructions. Make sure everyone knows what to do. Then have learners complete the activity. Have team reporters share their teams' ideas with the class.

4. Have partners read the Partner Work instructions. Make sure everyone knows what to do. Have learners complete the activity, switch partners, and repeat the activity. Ask a few pairs to present their dialogs to the class.

FOLLOW-UP

Checking Information: To help learners understand why it is important to confirm information before acting, have the class sit in a circle. Whisper a sentence of the dialog on this page into a learner's ear, then have learners continue to "pass" the sentence around the circle in this manner. The last learner should say the sentence aloud. Then read the original sentence to learners. Discuss what happened.

♦ Have learners repeat the activity, this time allowing each learner to confirm what he or she heard before repeating the sentence to the next learner. Have learners contrast the two experiences.

WORKBOOK

Unit 9, Exercise 3

WORKFORCE SKILLS (page 102)

Demonstrate leadership skills

★　　★　　★　　★　　★

SCANS Note

Suggest that learners should know how much authority they have at work. For example, if their manager is unavailable, what sorts of problems are they allowed to solve? What problems can they solve only with their manager's approval?

Personal Dictionary

Have learners add the words in their Personal Dictionary to their *Workforce Writing Dictionary*. For more information, see "Workforce Writing Dictionary" on page v.

Keep Talking　Taking action

 PRACTICE THE DIALOG

A The oven isn't working.

B What do you think we should do? Ms. Marshall's on vacation, so we can't ask her.

A Let's call the repair service. We have to have a working oven.

 PARTNER WORK

The manager's not at work today. Solve the problems. Tell your solutions to the class. Use the dialog above.

1. You get to work and find out the phones aren't working. The phones in the company next door are OK.

2. The company's most important customer is very upset because her latest order was missing several items. She needed those items today.

 Personal Dictionary ▸ Making Decisions

Write the words and phrases that you need to know.

_____

_____

102　　　　　　　　　　　　　　　　　　　　　　Unit 9

PREPARATION

Discuss problems learners have had at work when a manager wasn't around. What did they do? How did it turn out? Would they do the same thing or something different if the problem recurred?

PRESENTATION

1. Have learners read the Purpose Statement. See "Purpose Statement" on page viii.

 2. Focus attention on the photograph. Ask learners what they think the problem is. Write their ideas on the board and/or restate them in acceptable English. Then present the dialog. See "Presenting a Dialog" on page ix.

 3. Have partners read the Partner Work instructions. Make sure everyone knows what to do. Have learners complete the activity, switch partners, and repeat the activity. Have one or two pairs present their dialogs to the class.

4. Have learners read the Personal Dictionary instructions. Then use the Personal Dictionary procedures on page ix. Remind learners to continue to add words to their dictionaries throughout the unit.

FOLLOW-UP

TV News: Have teams present one of the Partner Work problems (or a problem at a team member's workplace) as a TV news spot. Ask teams to assign an anchor, a news reporter, and two or more workers. The anchor should introduce the news spot and, after it is over, summarize it. The reporter should interview the workers. Have teams act out their news spots for the class.

♦ Ask teams to talk about how team members respond to problems at work. Do they feel they have enough authority to take action? Do they feel they have too much authority? Have team reporters summarize discussions for the class.

WORKBOOK

Unit 9, Exercises 4A–4B

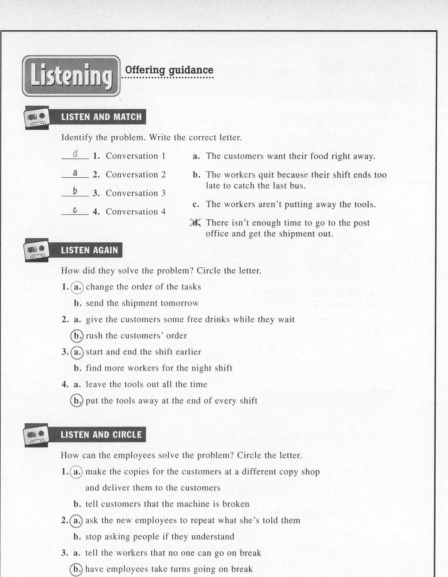

Listening — Offering guidance

LISTEN AND MATCH

Identify the problem. Write the correct letter.

_d_ **1.** Conversation 1
_a_ **2.** Conversation 2
_b_ **3.** Conversation 3
_c_ **4.** Conversation 4

a. The customers want their food right away.

b. The workers quit because their shift ends too late to catch the last bus.

c. The workers aren't putting away the tools.

d. There isn't enough time to go to the post office and get the shipment out.

LISTEN AGAIN

How did they solve the problem? Circle the letter.

1. (a.) change the order of the tasks
   b. send the shipment tomorrow

2. a. give the customers some free drinks while they wait
   (b.) rush the customers' order

3. (a.) start and end the shift earlier
   b. find more workers for the night shift

4. a. leave the tools out all the time
   (b.) put the tools away at the end of every shift

LISTEN AND CIRCLE

How can the employees solve the problem? Circle the letter.

1. (a.) make the copies for the customers at a different copy shop and deliver them to the customers
   b. tell customers that the machine is broken

2. (a.) ask the new employees to repeat what she's told them
   b. stop asking people if they understand

3. a. tell the workers that no one can go on break
   (b.) have employees take turns going on break

Unit 9

103

WORKFORCE SKILLS (page 103)

Demonstrate leadership skills

★   ★   ★   ★   ★

PREPARATION

To present or review **rush, packed,** and **shipment,** describe what you are doing as you act out getting a rush order out of the mailroom. Ask learners to describe times they had limited time to complete a task at work. What did they do?

PRESENTATION

1. Have learners read and discuss the Purpose Statement. For more information, see "Purpose Statement" on page viii.

 2. Have learners read the Listen and Match instructions. Make sure everyone understands the instructions. If necessary, model the first item. Then play the tape or read the Listening Transcript aloud two or more times as learners complete the activity. Have learners check their work. For more information, see "Presenting a Listening Activity" on page ix.

3. Have learners read the Listen Again instructions. Then follow the procedures in 2.

4. Have learners read the Listen and Circle instructions. Then follow the procedures in 2.

FOLLOW-UP

Offering Solutions: Have each team write a description of a work problem. Encourage teams to write about a problem at a team member's workplace. Then ask teams to exchange papers and discuss solutions to the problem they receive. Have team reporters share the problems and solutions with the class.

♦ Have learners work in pairs. Ask them to choose a problem one of the teams described and write a dialog in which two employees talk about how to solve it. Have several pairs read their dialogs to the class.

WORKBOOK

Unit 9, Exercise 5

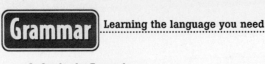

Learning the language you need

A. Study the Examples

> It's easy to change a tire.
> Changing a tire is easy.

COMPLETE THE SENTENCES

Use the language in A.

1. It's dangerous ____to smoke____ (**smoke**) at a gas station.

2. ____Finding____ (**Find**) time to learn a new skill can be difficult.

3. ____Working____ (**Work**) with people is what I enjoy most about my job.

4. It's important ____to wear____ (**wear**) safety shoes at the worksite.

5. ____Getting____ (**Get**) to work on time is easy now that I can drive.

6. It's required ____to wash____ (**wash**) your hands before you return to work.

REWRITE THE SENTENCES

Use the language in A.

1. It's expensive to eat lunch out every day.

   _____Eating lunch out every day is expensive._____

2. Walking to work is good exercise.

   _____It's good exercise to walk to work._____

3. It's interesting to drive a cab.

   _____Driving a cab is interesting._____

4. Driving downtown is sometimes dangerous.

   _____It's sometimes dangerous to drive downtown._____

104   Unit 9

PREPARATION

1. Review the language in the grammar boxes with learners before they open their books, if necessary.

2. Use picture cards to present or review **cab, luggage,** and **guests.** Use pantomime to present **greet** and **deliver.**

PRESENTATION

1. Have learners read and discuss the Purpose Statement. For more information, see "Purpose Statement" on page viii.

2. Have learners read the grammar box in A. Have learners use the language in the box to say as many sentences as possible. Tell learners that they can use the grammar box throughout the unit to review or check sentence structures.

3. Focus attention on Complete the Sentences. If necessary, model the first item. Then have learners complete the activity independently. Have a different learner read each sentence aloud while the rest of the class checks their answers.

4. Focus attention on Rewrite the Sentences. If necessary, model the first item. Then have learners complete the activity independently. Have a different learner read each sentence aloud while the rest of the class checks their answers.

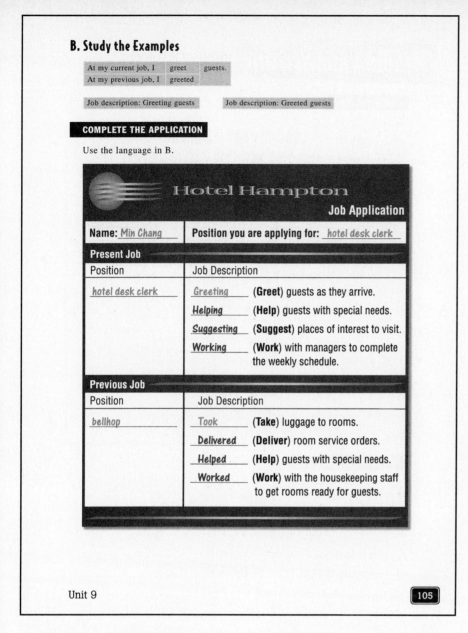

B. Study the Examples

| At my current job, I | greet | guests. |
| At my previous job, I | greeted | |

| Job description: Greeting guests | Job description: Greeted guests |

COMPLETE THE APPLICATION

Use the language in B.

Hotel Hampton
Job Application

Name: Min Chang   **Position you are applying for:** hotel desk clerk

Present Job

Position	Job Description
hotel desk clerk	Greeting (**Greet**) guests as they arrive.
	Helping (**Help**) guests with special needs.
	Suggesting (**Suggest**) places of interest to visit.
	Working (**Work**) with managers to complete the weekly schedule.

Previous Job

Position	Job Description
bellhop	Took (**Take**) luggage to rooms.
	Delivered (**Deliver**) room service orders.
	Helped (**Help**) guests with special needs.
	Worked (**Work**) with the housekeeping staff to get rooms ready for guests.

Unit 9   105

Language Note

Tell learners that they can use the language in B during job interviews. Suggest that they practice similar sentences about their current and past jobs before going to interviews.

5. Focus attention on the grammar boxes in B. Follow the procedures in 2.

6. Focus attention on Complete the Application. If necessary, model the first item. Then have learners complete the activity independently. Have a different learner read each answer aloud while the rest of the class checks their answers.

FOLLOW-UP

Job Experience: Have learners review the classified section of the newspaper and choose two jobs that interest them. Have learners imagine one job is their present job and the other is their past job. Then have them write lists of phrases describing their jobs, such as those in B. Have learners share their phrases with the class.

♦ To practice the language in grammar box A, go around the room and ask each learner in turn to complete a sentence that begins *It's dangerous to _____*. Then ask each learner to restate the sentence so it is in the form _____ *is dangerous*.

WORKBOOK

Unit 9, Exercises 6A–6C

BLACKLINE MASTERS

Blackline Master: Unit 9

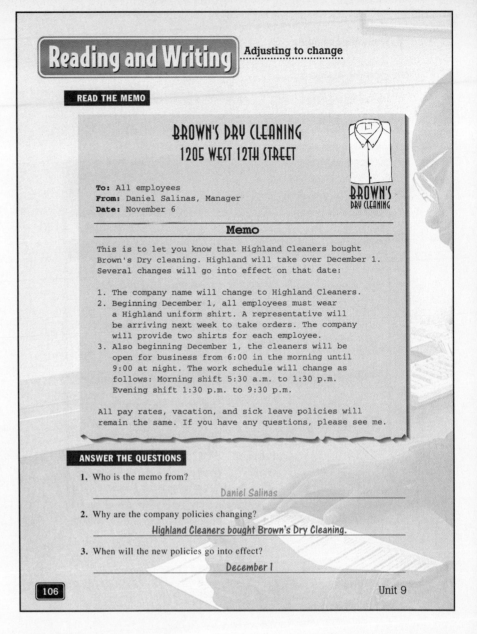

Reading and Writing ·········· Adjusting to change

READ THE MEMO

BROWN'S DRY CLEANING
1205 WEST 12TH STREET

To: All employees
From: Daniel Salinas, Manager
Date: November 6

BROWN'S DRY CLEANING

Memo

This is to let you know that Highland Cleaners bought Brown's Dry cleaning. Highland will take over December 1. Several changes will go into effect on that date:

1. The company name will change to Highland Cleaners.
2. Beginning December 1, all employees must wear a Highland uniform shirt. A representative will be arriving next week to take orders. The company will provide two shirts for each employee.
3. Also beginning December 1, the cleaners will be open for business from 6:00 in the morning until 9:00 at night. The work schedule will change as follows: Morning shift 5:30 a.m. to 1:30 p.m. Evening shift 1:30 p.m. to 9:30 p.m.

All pay rates, vacation, and sick leave policies will remain the same. If you have any questions, please see me.

ANSWER THE QUESTIONS

1. Who is the memo from?
   _____ *Daniel Salinas* _____

2. Why are the company policies changing?
   _____ *Highland Cleaners bought Brown's Dry Cleaning.* _____

3. When will the new policies go into effect?
   _____ *December 1* _____

106

Unit 9

PREPARATION

1. Use a picture card to present the word **uniform.** Ask learners to name professions in which employees wear uniforms.

2. Ask learners about times that big changes have occurred at their workplaces. Have them describe the experiences.

PRESENTATION

1. Have learners read and discuss the Purpose Statement. For more information, see "Purpose Statement" on page viii.

2. Have learners preview the memo. See "Prereading" on page x. Encourage learners to say everything they can about it. Write their ideas on the board

and/or restate them in acceptable English. Then have them read the memo independently.

3. Focus attention on Answer the Questions. Make sure everyone knows what to do. If necessary, model the first item on the board. Then have learners complete the activity independently. Have learners review each other's work in pairs. Ask several learners to share their answers with the class while the rest of the class checks their work.

You are an employee at the cleaners. Complete the chart to compare the old policies at Brown's Dry Cleaning to the new policies at Highland Cleaners.

Brown's Dry Cleaning (old policies)	Highland Cleaners (new policies)
1. Dress Code: Casual	**1.** Dress Code: *uniform shirts*
2. Hourly pay: $6.50	**2.** Hourly pay: *$6.50*
3. Morning Shift: 6:00 A.M. to 3:00 P.M.	**3.** Morning Shift: *5:30 A.M. to 1:30 P.M.*
Afternoon Shift: 3:00 P.M. to 9:30 P.M.	Afternoon Shift: *1:30 P.M. to 9:30 P.M.*
4. Sick days: 3	**4.** Sick days: *3*

TEAM WORK

Review the new policies. Why do you think Highland Cleaners changed the policies? Make a list with your team members. Talk about your team's views with the class.

 DISCUSSION

Have you ever experienced a policy change at your workplace or school? How did the changes affect you? Did you like the changes at first? later on? What did you do to adjust? Share your experiences with the class.

Unit 9   107

Culture Note

Explain that companies value workers who respond to change with a positive attitude. If a change causes problems, it is preferable to suggest solutions instead of complaining.

4. Focus attention on the illustration. Have learners say as much as they can about it. Help them identify the supervisor and the employee.

5. Have learners preview the chart. Follow the procedures in 2. Then have partners read the instructions for Write. Make sure everyone understands what to do. Then have learners complete the chart independently. Have several different learners read their responses aloud while the rest of the class checks their answers.

6. Have teams read the Team Work instructions. Make sure each team knows what to do. Then have teams complete the activity. Have team reporters talk about their teams' views with the class.

 **7.** Have learners read the Discussion questions. Then have them work in teams to discuss their ideas. Have team reporters summarize the discussions for the class.

FOLLOW-UP

Changes: Write on the board: *change in tools or equipment, change in job duties, change in management, and change in schedule.* Have teams discuss which type of change would be hardest for team members to adjust to in their particular jobs. Have them explain why. Ask team reporters to summarize the discussions for the class.

♦ Have teams make lists of strategies they could use to adjust to the changes they felt were hardest to adjust to. Have teams share their strategies with the class.

WORKBOOK

Unit 9, Exercises 7A–7B

Extension — Demonstrating leadership skills

READ THE ARTICLE

Workers Can Help Lead

Leadership helps companies improve. Workers can be leaders in many ways. Employees can make suggestions to make the company run better. This is what Kendra Lewis did for her company.

Cutting Down on Absenteeism

Kendra works for Harbor Foods. She's a team leader in a fish packing plant. Kendra works on the assembly line. She noticed that work on the line slowed down a lot toward the end of a shift. She also noticed that most workers who called in sick had back trouble or sore legs.

Kendra's legs were hurting a lot. She bought her team a special, comfortable mat to stand on, and soon everyone's legs felt better.

Kendra mentioned the mat to the plant manager, Mr. Marks. He thanked Kendra for the suggestion and bought mats for workers on all the teams at the plant. Records now show that production has gone up and fewer workers call in sick. Kendra's idea helped the company cut down on sick time and raise production.

TEAM WORK

Answer the questions. Share your answers with the class.

1. What was the problem at Harbor Foods? _Production was slow at the end of a shift, and workers missed work because of back trouble or sore legs._

2. What was Kendra's suggestion? _She suggested that the company buy special mats for the workers to stand on._

3. Did the suggestion help? Did Kendra show leadership? Why or why not? _Yes, the suggestion helped, and Kendra showed leadership by making a suggestion that helped the company run better._

 TEAM WORK

Talk about a problem at your workplace that you can solve.

 Culture Notes

When are leadership skills important at your workplace or school? What happens to employees who are good leaders?

108   Unit 9

PREPARATION

To present or review **absenteeism,** use the word in several sample sentences. Ask if absenteeism is a problem at learners' workplaces. Encourage learners to use the new language in their answers.

PRESENTATION

1. Have learners read and discuss the Purpose Statement. See "Purpose Statement" on page viii.

2. Have learners preview the article. See "Prereading" on page x. Encourage them to say everything they can about it. Write learners' ideas on the board and/or restate them in acceptable English. Then have learners read the article independently.

3. Have teams read the Team Work instructions. Make sure each team knows what to do. Then have teams complete the activity. Have team reporters share their answers with the class.

 4. Focus attention on the Team Work instructions and then follow the procedures in 3.

 **5.** Have learners read Culture Notes and talk over their responses in teams. Have team reporters share their ideas with the class. Ask the teams to compare each other's ideas. See "Culture Notes" on page vii.

FOLLOW-UP

What Makes a Leader? Distribute help wanted pages from newspapers to each team. Ask teams to circle several management positions in the ads, such as restaurant managers or management trainees. Have learners list general skills that these jobs require. Have team reporters share their lists with the class.

♦ Ask partners to talk about their leadership skills. What do they do well? What would they have to do better to be leaders at their jobs? Have one or two pairs share their dialogs with the class.

WORKBOOK

Unit 9, Exercise 8

Performance Check — How well can you use the skills in this unit?

Complete the activities. Go over your work with a partner or your teacher. Then complete the Performance Review on page 110.

SKILL 1 CONFIRM INFORMATION BEFORE YOU ACT

Circle the letter.

1. A waiter told the restaurant manager that the cooks keep giving him cold food. What should the manager do first?

   a. complain to the cooks

   (b.) check the food as it leaves the kitchen

2. A supermarket customer told the supermarket manager that none of the milk is fresh. What should the manager do first?

   a. speak with the milk stockers

   (b.) check the milk

SKILL 2 DEMONSTRATE LEADERSHIP SKILLS

NEEDED: LEADERSHIP

Last year many customers at Ming's Chinese Restaurant were unhappy. They said that their food was cold when it arrived. Liu Min, manager of the restaurant, saw that sometimes waiters didn't notice when food was ready. It would sit in the kitchen for several minutes. As a result, the food got cold. Ms. Liu got a small bell for cooks to ring when an order is ready. When the waiters hear the bell, they go to the kitchen to get the food while it's hot.

Read the article and answer the questions on a sheet of paper. Share your answers with a partner or your teacher.

1. What was the problem at Ming's Chinese Restaurant?

2. What did Liu Min do? Did she solve the problem? Explain whether or not she showed good leadership skills.

Unit 9

109

PRESENTATION

Use any of the procedures in "Evaluation," page x, with pages 109 and 110. Record individuals' results on the Unit 9 Individual Competency Chart. Record the class's results on the Class Cumulative Competency Chart.

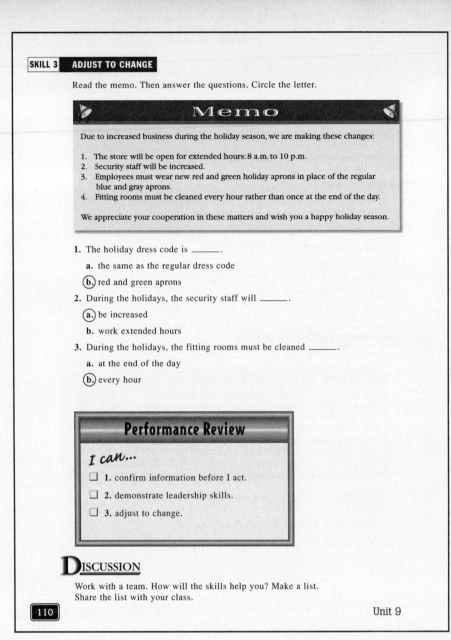

SKILL 3 ADJUST TO CHANGE

Read the memo. Then answer the questions. Circle the letter.

Memo

Due to increased business during the holiday season, we are making these changes:

1. The store will be open for extended hours: 8 a.m. to 10 p.m.
2. Security staff will be increased.
3. Employees must wear new red and green holiday aprons in place of the regular blue and gray aprons.
4. Fitting rooms must be cleaned every hour rather than once at the end of the day.

We appreciate your cooperation in these matters and wish you a happy holiday season.

1. The holiday dress code is _____.

  a. the same as the regular dress code

  b. red and green aprons

2. During the holidays, the security staff will _____.

  a. be increased

  b. work extended hours

3. During the holidays, the fitting rooms must be cleaned _____.

  a. at the end of the day

  b. every hour

Performance Review

I can...

☐ 1. confirm information before I act.

☐ 2. demonstrate leadership skills.

☐ 3. adjust to change.

DISCUSSION

Work with a team. How will the skills help you? Make a list.
Share the list with your class.

110   Unit 9

PRESENTATION

Follow the instructions on page 109.

INFORMAL WORKPLACE-SPECIFIC ASSESSMENT

Ask learners to explain how they will demonstrate leadership skills at work in the future.

WORKBOOK

Unit 9, Exercise 9

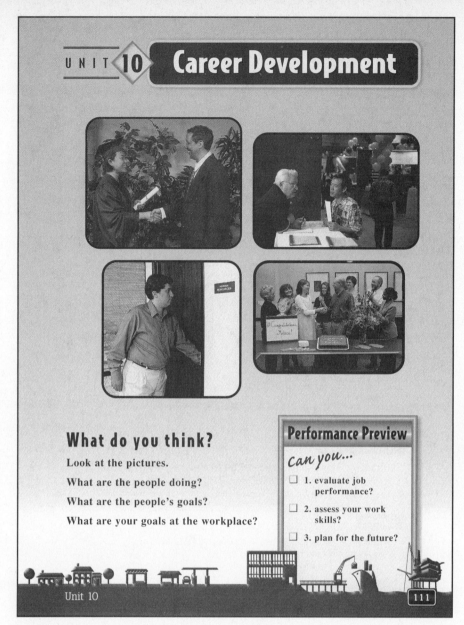

Unit 10 Overview
—SCANS Competencies—

★ Acquire and evaluate data

★ Allocate time

★ Understand organizational systems

★ Monitor performance

Workforce Skills

- Evaluate job performance
- Assess your work skills
- Plan for the future

Materials

- Sample of an inventory report
- Help wanted ads; class listings for local community colleges
- Picture cards of a shipping department and an electronics assembler
- Blank performance review forms

Unit Warm-Up

To get the learners thinking about the unit topic (personal work goals), share the key steps that resulted in your becoming a teacher, such as setting your goal, graduating, and interviewing for the job. Have learners share their work goals.

★　　★　　★　　★　　★

WORKFORCE SKILLS (page 111)

Assess your work skills

★　　★　　★　　★　　★

PREPARATION

Explain that **job performance** refers to how well an employee does his or her job. Ask learners to name some benefits that might result from good job performance, such as pay raises and increased responsibility.

PRESENTATION

1. Focus attention on the photographs. Ask learners what they think the unit might be about. Write their ideas on the board and/or restate them in acceptable English.

2. Ask learners to explain how the people in the photographs are developing their careers. Have volunteers describe similar experiences they have had.

3. Help learners read the questions. Discuss the questions with the class.

4. You may want to use the Performance Preview to provide learners with an overview of the skills in the unit. Have learners read the list of skills and discuss what they will learn in the unit.

FOLLOW-UP

Sharing Information: On the board, list each learner's current and past jobs. Then have learners talk to classmates with experience in a job that interests them. The "consultants" should describe

what they do at work and answer questions. Have one or two learners talk about what they learned.

♦ Have each learner write a list of things they learned about the job they are interested in. Have several learners read their lists to the class.

WORKBOOK

Unit 10, Exercise 1

Assess your work skills

Plan for the future

★　　★　　★　　★　　★

Teaching Note

Use this page to introduce the new language in the unit. Whenever possible, encourage peer teaching. Supply any language learners need.

SCANS Note

Suggest that before learners go on a job interview, they think about which of their skills are relevant to that job, then focus on those skills during the interview. As an example, ask learners if job applicants should talk about their driving skills when applying for a job as a cook. What skills should they talk about?

Getting Started
Identifying work skills

TEAM WORK

Look at the pictures. What skills do the workers have? Write the letter. What other skills do you think they have? Tell your team.

Delivery Driver

Cashier

Forklift Operator

Housekeeper

a. I can count money and make change accurately.
b. I have good driving skills, and I know how the warehouse is organized.
c. I'm very organized. I know the city's streets and neighborhoods.
d. I can clean rooms. I can follow written instructions.

PARTNER WORK

The people in the pictures want to get better jobs. Take turns saying jobs the people can get with their present skills.

A The cashier is good at counting money. He can get a job as a bank teller.

SURVEY

What kind of job would you like to have in five years? As a class, make a list of everyone's career goals.

112   Unit 10

PREPARATION

To clarify **accurate** and **organized,** act out each word and its opposite. For example, draw a line on the board. Give its length in vague terms, then in precise inches. Identify the precise measure as **accurate.**

PRESENTATION

1. Have learners read and discuss the Purpose Statement. See "Purpose Statement" on page viii.

2. Focus attention on the illustrations. Encourage learners to say as much as they can about them. Write their ideas on the board and/or restate them in acceptable English.

3. Have teams read the Team Work instructions. Make sure each team knows what to do. Then have teams complete the activity. Have team reporters share their answers with the class.

4. Have partners read the Partner Work instructions. Make sure partners know what to do. If necessary, model the activity. Then have partners complete the activity, switch partners, and repeat the activity. Have one or two partners present their dialogs to the class.

5. Have learners read the Survey instructions. Make sure each learner knows what to do. If necessary, model the activity. Then have learners complete the activity. Have learners share their career goals with the class. See "Survey" on page viii.

FOLLOW-UP

Five Year Plans: Have learners list the skills they need to reach their five-year career goals. Have a few learners read their lists to the class.

♦ Have learners work in teams. Each team member should draw a five-year time line with his or her current job at one end and a five-year career goal at the other. The rest of the team should suggest training programs or intermediate jobs to add to the years in between. Post the time lines in the classroom.

WORKBOOK

Unit 10, Exercises 2A–2B

---

112   English ASAP

　Assessing your work skills

PRACTICE THE DIALOG

A Thank you for letting me help out on that inventory report. I really enjoyed it.

B I'm glad to hear that. Everyone said your work was excellent.

A Thanks. I've always been good with numbers.

B Have you ever thought about a career working with numbers?

A Yes, I think I'd like to be an accountant someday. In fact, last month I started studying business math at the community college.

B You might want to talk to someone in our accounting department about a job when your classes are finished. They often hire students from the college.

Now, describe your job skills to your partner. Point out which skill you do best. Use the dialog and the Useful Language above.

ASAP PROJECT

As a class make a list of resources such as employment offices, human resource departments, schools, and the public library, where you can get information on career development. The list should include addresses and phone numbers. Complete this project as you work through the unit.

Unit 10

113

Tip To get a promotion, find out what openings are available at your workplace. Then get the training or experience you need to apply for the job you want.

Useful Language

I'm good at . . .

I'm a good . . .

I'm best at . . .

Language Note

Explain that, while most adjectives add **-er** *or* **-est** *to compare two or more objects, the word* **good** *becomes* **better** *when comparing two items and* **best** *when comparing three or more. Show learners two objects and ask which they like better and why. Repeat for* **best** *with three or more objects.*

ASAP PROJECT

Have learners read the instructions. Discuss the project and its purpose with learners. Make sure that everyone understands. Throughout the rest of the unit, allow time for learners to work on the project, supplying information from personal experience or research. Have the class agree on a deadline when the project will be finished. See "ASAP Project" on page vi.

PREPARATION

Use realia or a sample to present **inventory report.** Explain that an **accountant** works with numbers, for example, to prepare company financial reports. Ask learners what they like or dislike about working with numbers.

PRESENTATION

1. Have learners read and discuss the Purpose Statement. For more information, see "Purpose Statement" on page viii.

 2. Focus attention on the photograph. Encourage learners to say as much as they can about it. Have them identify the supervisor and decide whether or not she seems pleased with the other employee's work. Write learners' ideas

on the board and/or restate them in acceptable English. Then present the dialog. See "Presenting a Dialog" on page ix.

3. Have partners read the instructions under the dialog. Make sure everyone understands what to do. Then focus attention on the Useful Language box. Help learners read the expressions. If necessary, model pronunciation. Then have learners complete the activity, switch partners, and repeat several times. Ask a few partners to present their dialogs to the class.

Tip Have learners read the Tip independently. Have them discuss how the advice will help them. See "Presenting a Tip" on page ix.

FOLLOW-UP

Work Skills: Have team members describe their talents, interests, and skills to each other. The team should respond by suggesting jobs that would be a good match. Have team reporters share their teams' ideas with the class.

♦ Have teams look through help wanted ads for additional jobs that could match team members' interests and skills. Have team reporters summarize what the teams found for the class.

WORKBOOK

Unit 10, Exercises 3A–3B

★   ★   ★   ★   ★

SCANS Note

Encourage learners to share with their managers their career goals, even those in the distant future. Recommend that they ask for advice about improving their existing skills, acquiring new skills, and achieving their goals.

Personal Dictionary

Have learners add the words in their Personal Dictionary to their *Workforce Writing Dictionary.* For more information, see "Workforce Writing Dictionary" on page v.

Keep Talking · · · Planning for the future

 PRACTICE THE DIALOG

A I'd like to apply for a delivery driver's job.

B You're one of the best workers on the loading dock. Why do you want to change jobs?

A I'm interested in having a little more responsibility.

B You need a commercial driver's license to get that job. Do you have one?

A No, not yet. I plan to sign up for a class next month.

B Good thinking. Check with Human Resources. Usually the company will pay for the class.

 Tip
Education is a good way to prepare for a better job. Find out if your company will pay for your classes.

PARTNER WORK

Think about a job you would like to have. Tell your partner why you want the job and what you need to do to get it. Use the dialog above and the Useful Language.

Useful Language

I'd like to . . .

I want to . . .

I'm planning to . . .

I hope to . . .

Personal Dictionary ▷ Getting a Better Job

Write the words and phrases that you need to know.

_____

_____

_____

Unit 10

PREPARATION

Display class listings or a course catalog from a local community college or training center. Indicate classes that teach work skills, such as computer classes, business classes, or specific job-related classes. Ask learners how taking classes can help workers advance.

PRESENTATION

1. Have learners read the Purpose Statement. See "Purpose Statement" on page viii.

 2. Focus attention on the illustration. Have learners say as much as they can about it. Write their ideas on the board and/or restate them in acceptable English. Then present the dialog. See "Presenting a

Dialog" on page ix.

 3. Have partners read the Partner Work instructions. Focus attention on the Useful Language box. Help learners read the expressions. Have learners complete the activity, switch partners, and repeat. Have a few pairs present their dialogs to the class.

4. Have learners read the Personal Dictionary instructions. Then use the Personal Dictionary procedures on page ix. Remind learners to continue to add words to their dictionaries throughout the unit.

Tip Have learners read the Tip independently. Have them discuss how the advice will help them. See "Presenting a Tip" on page ix.

FOLLOW-UP

Take the Next Step: Have partners look through a catalog or class list and choose classes that could help them at work. Have them discuss these questions: *What skills will I gain? What skills do I need before I take the class? How soon will the class help me at work?* Have pairs share their ideas with the class.

♦ Ask partners to find the information that explains how to register for the class and tells what the class will cost. Have several learners describe the procedures and fees to the class.

WORKBOOK

Unit 10, Exercise 4

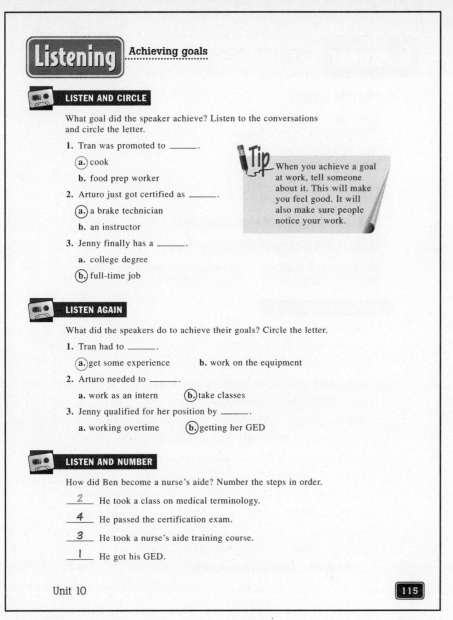

PREPARATION

Explain that when employees are **certified** for a job, they've completed the officially required training. Use the words **promoted** and **raise** in several sample sentences.

PRESENTATION

1. Have learners read and discuss the Purpose Statement. See "Purpose Statement" on page viii.

 2. Have learners read the Listen and Circle instructions. Make sure everyone knows what to do. If necessary, model the first item. Then play the tape or read the Listening Transcript aloud two or more times as learners complete the activity. Have learners check their work. See "Presenting a Listening Activity" on page ix.

 3. Have learners read the Listen Again instructions. Then follow the procedures in 2.

 4. Have learners read the Listen and Number instructions. Then follow the procedures in 2.

Tip Have learners read the Tip independently. Have learners discuss how the advice will help them. For more information, see "Presenting a Tip" on page ix.

FOLLOW-UP

Moving up to Manager: Cut descriptions of managerial jobs from help wanted ads and distribute one ad to each team. Ask teams to discuss ways a worker could acquire the experience and skills for a promotion to the managerial position. Have teams share their ideas.

♦ Ask learners to list their accomplishments at work or at school. Have volunteers share their lists with the class.

WORKBOOK

Unit 10, Exercise 5

Assess your work skills

Plan for the future

★   ★   ★   ★   ★

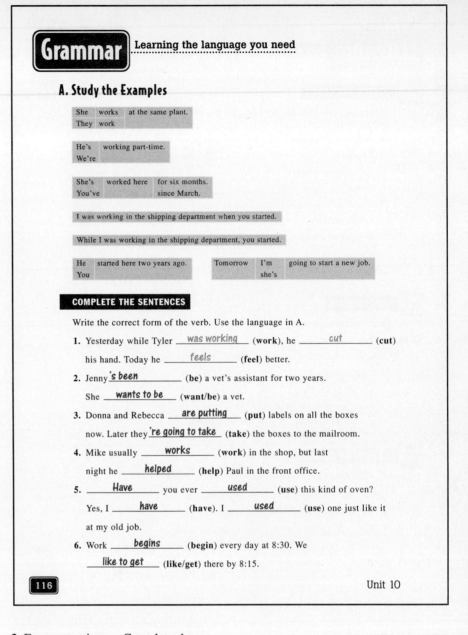

Grammar — Learning the language you need

A. Study the Examples

| She | works | at the same plant. |
| They | work | |

| He's | working part-time. |
| We're | |

| She's | worked here | for six months. |
| You've | | since March. |

I was working in the shipping department when you started.

While I was working in the shipping department, you started.

| He | started here two years ago. |
| You | |

| Tomorrow | I'm | going to start a new job. |
| | she's | |

COMPLETE THE SENTENCES

Write the correct form of the verb. Use the language in A.

1. Yesterday while Tyler ___was working___ (**work**), he ___cut___ (**cut**)
   his hand. Today he ___feels___ (**feel**) better.

2. Jenny ___'s been___ (**be**) a vet's assistant for two years.
   She ___wants to be___ (**want/be**) a vet.

3. Donna and Rebecca ___are putting___ (**put**) labels on all the boxes
   now. Later they ___'re going to take___ (**take**) the boxes to the mailroom.

4. Mike usually ___works___ (**work**) in the shop, but last
   night he ___helped___ (**help**) Paul in the front office.

5. ___Have___ you ever ___used___ (**use**) this kind of oven?
   Yes, I ___have___ (**have**). I ___used___ (**use**) one just like it
   at my old job.

6. Work ___begins___ (**begin**) every day at 8:30. We
   ___like to get___ (**like/get**) there by 8:15.

116   Unit 10

PREPARATION

Review the language in the grammar boxes with learners before they open their books, if necessary. Use picture cards to present or review **shipping department** and **electronics assembler.**

PRESENTATION

1. Have learners read and discuss the Purpose Statement. For more information, see "Purpose Statement" on page viii.

2. Have learners read the grammar boxes in A. Have them use the language in the boxes to say as many sentences as possible. Tell learners that they can use the grammar boxes throughout the unit to review or check sentence structures.

3. Focus attention on Complete the Sentences. If necessary, model the first item on the board. Then have learners complete the activity independently. Have a different learner read each sentence aloud while the rest of the class checks their answers.

WRITE

Complete Lorenzo Rey's story. Write the correct form of the verb.

1. In 1978, he ___arrived___ (**arrive**) in New York. Later he ___moved___ (**move**) to Boston. He___'s lived___ (**live**) in Boston since 1985. His address ___is___ (**be**) 159 River Street.

2. He ___got___ (**get**) a job at Best Industries five years ago. When he ___started___ (**start**) working there, he ___was___ (**be**) a janitor. Now he___'s___ (**be**) an electronics assembler. He ___makes___ (**make**) computer parts. He ___likes___ (**like**) his job.

3. Today Lorenzo Rey ___isn't___ (**not be**) at work. He___'s___ (**be**) sick. Later today he___'s going to go___ (**go**) to the doctor.

WRITE

Tell about yourself. Use the language above as a model. Write your sentences on a sheet of paper.

Unit 10   117

---

4. Focus attention on Write. Discuss the illustrations. Have learners say as much as they can about them. Then follow the procedures in 3.

5. Focus attention on Write. Make sure everyone knows what to do. Then have learners complete the activity. Check learners' work. Ask several learners to read their sentences to the class.

FOLLOW-UP

Asking and Answering: Have partners talk about their current and previous jobs by asking and answering questions such as: *Where do you work now? When did you start working there? What time do you begin? Are you working anywhere else?* Ask several pairs to present their dialogs to the class.

♦ Ask partners to write their dialogs. Check learners' work.

WORKBOOK
Unit 10, Exercises 6A–6C

BLACKLINE MASTERS
Blackline Master: Unit 10

★　　★　　★　　★　　★

Reading and Writing

Evaluating job performance

READ THE PERFORMANCE REVIEW

EMPLOYEE PERFORMANCE REVIEW

NAME: Mary Jones	**JOB TITLE:** Cashier
DEPARTMENT: Customer Service	

JOB RESPONSIBILITIES	5 is the highest rating. 1 is the lowest.
1. ATTITUDE: Demonstrates a positive overall attitude toward the workplace, coworkers, and job duties.	1　　2　　③　　4　　5 Explanation: _Mary enjoys working with customers. She has a good attitude toward the workplace and her job duties. However, she doesn't want to help her coworkers._
2. SKILLS: Understands and executes job skills appropriately and in a timely manner.	1　　2　　3　　④　　5 Explanation: _Mary is fast on the cash register and always gives correct change. She helps customers quickly and professionally. Her checkstand is always neat, and she always finishes her duties on time._
3. TEAM PARTICIPATION: Assists other employees in learning job tasks. Works well with others. Helps in other areas when needed.	1　　②　　3　　4　　5 Explanation: _Mary complains when she is asked to help out in the stock room._
OVERALL RATING	1　　2　　3　　4　　5

WRITE THE ANSWER

1. Which category did Mary Jones have the highest rating in? _____ Skills

2. Which category does Mary Jones need to improve most?
   Team Participation

3. What suggestion would you give Mary Jones to improve her job performance?
   Develop a better attitude toward teams and helping coworkers.

PARTNER WORK

What overall rating do you think Mary Jones should receive? Circle the number in the review and give an explanation. Then make a plan for how Mary Jones can improve her performance.

118

Unit 10

Culture Note

Tell learners that one way to improve performance is to find a "role model" or "mentor" among their coworkers— usually an older and/or more experienced employee that they admire. Learners can emulate the exemplary behavior of their role models and ask them for advice.

PREPARATION

To teach or review the new phrases on these pages, role-play a boss conducting a performance review. Include the phrases **team participation** and **positive overall attitude,** giving examples of each. Ask volunteers to describe performance reviews at their workplaces.

PRESENTATION

1. Have learners read and discuss the Purpose Statement. For more information, see "Purpose Statement" on page viii.

2. Have learners preview the performance review. See "Prereading" on page x. Encourage learners to say everything they can about it. Write their ideas on the board and/or restate them in acceptable English. Then have them read the performance review independently.

3. Focus attention on Write the Answer. Make sure everyone knows what to do. If necessary, model an item on the board. Then have learners complete the activity independently. Ask several learners to share their answers with the class while the rest of the class checks their work.

4. Have partners read the Partner Work instructions. Make sure everyone understands what to do. Then have learners complete the activity, switch partners, and repeat. Have one or two partners present their explanations and plans to the class.

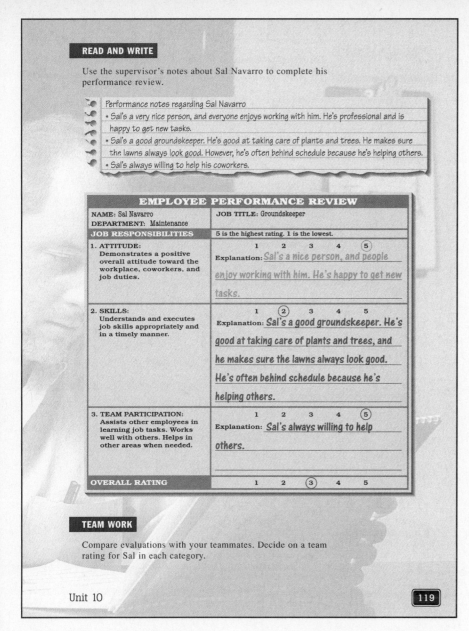

READ AND WRITE

Use the supervisor's notes about Sal Navarro to complete his performance review.

> Performance notes regarding Sal Navarro
> • Sal's a very nice person, and everyone enjoys working with him. He's professional and is happy to get new tasks.
> • Sal's a good groundskeeper. He's good at taking care of plants and trees. He makes sure the lawns always look good. However, he's often behind schedule because he's helping others.
> • Sal's always willing to help his coworkers.

EMPLOYEE PERFORMANCE REVIEW

NAME: Sal Navarro DEPARTMENT: Maintenance	JOB TITLE: Groundskeeper
JOB RESPONSIBILITIES	5 is the highest rating. 1 is the lowest.
1. ATTITUDE: Demonstrates a positive overall attitude toward the workplace, coworkers, and job duties.	1 2 3 4 ⑤ Explanation: Sal's a nice person, and people enjoy working with him. He's happy to get new tasks.
2. SKILLS: Understands and executes job skills appropriately and in a timely manner.	1 ② 3 4 5 Explanation: Sal's a good groundskeeper. He's good at taking care of plants and trees, and he makes sure the lawns always look good. He's often behind schedule because he's helping others.
3. TEAM PARTICIPATION: Assists other employees in learning job tasks. Works well with others. Helps in other areas when needed.	1 2 3 4 ⑤ Explanation: Sal's always willing to help others.
OVERALL RATING	1 2 ③ 4 5

TEAM WORK

Compare evaluations with your teammates. Decide on a team rating for Sal in each category.

Unit 10

119

Teaching Note

You might have learners complete Read and Write in pairs.

---

5. Have learners preview the notes and review form. Follow the procedures in 2.

6. Have partners read the instructions for Read and Write. Make sure everyone understands what to do. Model if necessary. Then have learners complete the activity independently. Have several different learners read their review forms aloud while the rest of the class checks their answers.

7. Have teams read the Team Work instructions. Make sure each team knows what to do. Then have teams complete the activity. Have team reporters share their ratings with the class.

FOLLOW-UP

Evaluations: Have pairs role-play performance evaluations. Partners should take turns as the "employer" and evaluate the "employee" as if he or she works where they do.

♦ Give learners blank Employee Performance Review forms. Ask them to write up the review they just gave their "employee." Have several learners read their evaluations to the class.

WORKBOOK

Unit 10, Exercises 7A–7B

WORKFORCE SKILLS (page 120)

Assess your work skills

★　　★　　★　　★　　★

Extension ·· Using self assessment to make career choices

COMPLETE THE ASSESSMENT

Work Values Assessment

Do the statements describe your work values?
Write yes or no.

_____ 1. I enjoy working with my hands.

_____ 2. I enjoy working with machines and equipment.

_____ 3. I like moving from place to place while I work.

_____ 4. I like math and numbers.

_____ 5. I like to help people.

Circle the words that best describe your work values.

6. I (**like / do not like**) working with customers.

7. I would rather work (**alone / in a group**).

8. I enjoy (**variety / routine**) in my workday.

9. I prefer working (**indoors / outdoors**).

10. I prefer working with (**adults / children**).

ANSWER THE QUESTIONS

1. Name at least three jobs that match most of your assessed values.

   <u>Answers will vary.</u>

2. Which of the jobs would you choose? Why?

   _____

3. Which main work values influenced your choice?

   _____

 Culture Notes

You are thinking about transferring to a better job in another department at your workplace. What do you say to your current boss? Talk about ways to get support for changing jobs.

120   Unit 10

PREPARATION

Ask learners a series of questions, such as *Which is more important to you, the shift you work or the people you work with?* Explain that the answers tell something about their **work values,** or what's most important to them in a job.

PRESENTATION

1. Have learners read and discuss the Purpose Statement. See "Purpose Statement" on page viii.

2. Have learners preview the values assessment form. Encourage learners to say everything they can about it. Write their ideas on the board and/or restate them in acceptable English.

3. Focus attention on Complete the Assessment. Make sure everyone understands what to do. Then have learners complete the activity independently. Have several learners read their forms aloud.

4. Focus attention on Answer the Questions. Make sure everyone understands what to do. Then have learners complete the activity independently. Discuss learners' answers as a class.

 **5.** Have learners read Culture Notes and talk over their responses in teams. Have team reporters share their ideas with the class. Ask the teams to compare each other's ideas. See "Culture Notes" on page vii.

FOLLOW-UP

Values Match: Distribute copies of help wanted ads. Ask learners to circle three or more ads for jobs that match their work values. Have volunteers share their work values and the jobs they circled.

◆ Ask partners to talk about career choices they made because of their work values, asking and answering questions such as: *Which of your values did the job match? Which didn't it match?* Have one or two pairs share their dialogs with the class.

WORKBOOK

Unit 10, Exercise 8

How well can you use the skills in this unit?

Complete the activities. Go over your work with a partner or your teacher. Then complete the Performance Review on page 122.

SKILL 1	EVALUATE JOB PERFORMANCE

Read the supervisor's notes and complete the evaluation.

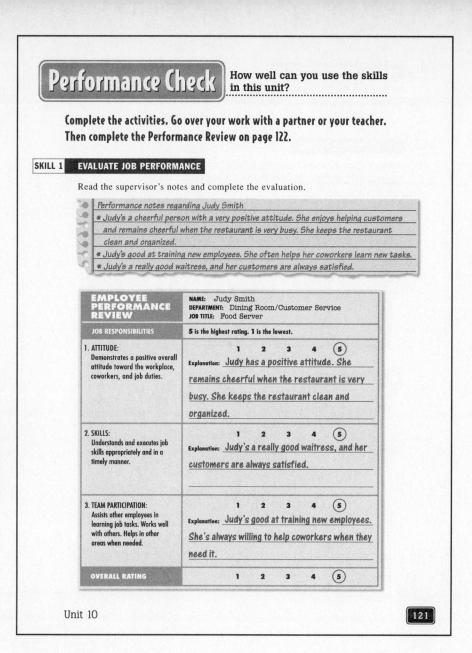

Performance notes regarding Judy Smith
* Judy's a cheerful person with a very positive attitude. She enjoys helping customers and remains cheerful when the restaurant is very busy. She keeps the restaurant clean and organized.
* Judy's good at training new employees. She often helps her coworkers learn new tasks.
* Judy's a really good waitress, and her customers are always satisfied.

EMPLOYEE PERFORMANCE REVIEW

NAME: Judy Smith
DEPARTMENT: Dining Room/Customer Service
JOB TITLE: Food Server

JOB RESPONSIBILITIES — 5 is the highest rating. 1 is the lowest.

1. ATTITUDE: Demonstrates a positive overall attitude toward the workplace, coworkers, and job duties.
   1 2 3 4 (5)
   Explanation: Judy has a positive attitude. She remains cheerful when the restaurant is very busy. She keeps the restaurant clean and organized.

2. SKILLS: Understands and executes job skills appropriately and in a timely manner.
   1 2 3 4 (5)
   Explanation: Judy's a really good waitress, and her customers are always satisfied.

3. TEAM PARTICIPATION: Assists other employees in learning job tasks. Works well with others. Helps in other areas when needed.
   1 2 3 4 (5)
   Explanation: Judy's good at training new employees. She's always willing to help coworkers when they need it.

OVERALL RATING
   1 2 3 4 (5)

Unit 10   121

PRESENTATION

Use any of the procedures in "Evaluation," page x, with pages 121 and 122. Record individuals' results on the Unit 10 Individual Competency Chart. Record the class's results on the Class Cumulative Competency Chart.

PRESENTATION

Follow the instructions on page 121.

INFORMAL WORKPLACE-SPECIFIC ASSESSMENT

Ask learners to tell you their career
goals and describe steps they can take
to achieve them.

WORKBOOK

Unit 10, Exercise 9

Vocabulary

 **U N I T 1**

fill out
find out

who
what
where
when
why
how

 **U N I T 2**

duties
experience
skills

important

depend on
transfer

 U N I T 3

bar code
computer
debit card
enter
printout
scanner
screen

price
track
weigh

 U N I T 4

priority
setback

prioritize
procrastinate
put off

long-term goal
short-term goal

 **U N I T 5**

apology
complaint
guidelines
solution

apologize
respond
solve

U N I T 6

boss
coworkers
supervisor
manager

U N I T 7

budget
expense
income
insurance
labor
rent
utilities

 **U N I T 8**

sit up
clean up
lift

diet
exercise
injury
sleep
stress

U N I T 9

change
check
complain
solve
take action

policy
solution
problem

U N I T 10

goal
performance review
skill

Irregular Verbs

am, are, is	was, were	been
begin	began	begun
break	broke	broken
bring	brought	brought
build	built	built
buy	bought	bought
come	came	come
cut	cut	cut
do	did	done
drive	drove	driven
eat	ate	eaten
feed	fed	fed
feel	felt	felt
find	found	found
forget	forgot	forgotten
get	got	gotten
give	gave	given
go	went	went
have	had	had
keep	kept	kept
made	made	made
pay	paid	paid
put	put	put
read	read	read
ride	rode	ridden
see	saw	seen
sell	sold	sold
send	sent	sent
speak	spoke	spoken
spend	spent	spent
sweep	swept	swept
take	took	taken
tell	told	told
think	thought	thought
wear	wore	worn
write	wrote	written

Work Histories

Steven Cho	Mark Johnson
delivery driver, 1998–1999	house cleaner, 1996–1998
taxi driver, 1999–present	office cleaner, 1998–present
Andrea Wolfe	**Ahmed Siam**
hospital cook, 1995–1997	toy sales clerk, 1998–1999
nursing home cook, 1997–present	shoe sales clerk, 1999–present

A. Complete the sentences. Use the work histories. Follow the examples.

1. Andrea _____*used to cook*_____ (**cook**) at a hospital.

2. Andrea _____*cooks*_____ (**cook**) at a nursing home.

3. Steven _____ (**drive**) a taxi.

4. Steven _____ (**drive**) a delivery truck.

5. Ahmed _____ (**sell**) toys.

6. Ahmed _____ (**sell**) shoes.

7. Mark _____ (**clean**) offices.

8. Mark _____ (**clean**) houses.

B. Complete the sentences. Follow the examples.

1. While I ___*was washing*___ (**wash**) the car, the rain _____*started*_____ (**start**).

2. When the customer _____ (**arrive**), I _____ (**clean**) the counters.

3. While Tony _____ (**count**) the money in the cash register, Donna _____ (**turn off**) the lights in the front of the store.

4. When Marco _____ (**fall**), he _____ (**unload**) the truck.

5. When the alarm clock _____ (**ring**), Laura _____ (**sleep**).

C. Complete the sentences. Write the correct form of the word.

1. Last year we _____stayed_____ (stay) open late for holiday shoppers.

2. Rita _____ (take) a cooking class last year.

3. We _____ (not finish) the inventory yesterday.

4. Mark _____ (take) the truck to the garage last week.

5. We _____ (tell) the customer that we would finish early this morning.

6. Diane _____ (sew) new buttons on the blouse.

7. They _____ (finish) the walls yesterday before they

   _____ (start) the floor.

8. The technicians _____ (not fix) the computer yesterday. They

   _____ (buy) new parts but _____

   (not install) them.

9. Last week we _____ (get) the new washing machines.

10. Last month Tony _____ (not write) the schedule. Lisa

    _____ (write) it.

D. Read Sam's to do list. Complete the report. Follow the example.

Sam,

Please do the things on this list today. Write a report telling me what you did and leave it on my desk.

Thanks,

Philip

1. Take out the trash.
2. Sweep the front sidewalk.
3. Go to the electric company's office and pay the bill.
4. Find the missing tools.
5. Make 100 copies of the sales flier.
6. Mop the floor.
7. Fix the sink in the ladies' rest room.

If you have time, change the lock on the back door. The hardware is in the store room.

Philip,

Thanks for the list. Here's what I did.

I __took out__ the trash.

I _____ the front sidewalk.

I _____ to the electric company's

office and _____ the bill.

I _____ the missing tools.

I _____ copies of the sales flier.

I _____ the floor and _____

the sink in the ladies' rest room.

Tomorrow I'm going to change the lock on the back door.

Sam

Name _____

A. Complete the sentences. Use the words in the word box. Follow the example.

hungry   happy   disappointed   ~~upset~~   tired

1. Greg is late to work. He probably _____*feels upset*_____.

2. Tina and I ordered a large pizza for lunch. We _____.

3. Mary's boss just told her she is doing a good job.

   She probably _____.

4. The workers just found out they won't get a bonus this month.

   They probably _____.

5. Rick worked two shifts yesterday. That's why he _____.

B. Complete the sentences. Follow the examples.

1. Alice _____*takes*_____ (**take**) the bus to work every day.

   Right now she __*'s waiting*_____ (**wait**) for the 157 bus.

2. Every day Ben _____ (**make**) lunch for the children

   at Washington School. He_____ (**cook**) lunch right now.

3. Mary _____ (**work**) as a cashier.

   She_____ (**ring up**) a sale now.

4. Marta _____ (**help**) in the kitchen on Tuesdays.

   Right now she_____ (**prepare**) fruit salad.

5. Tina _____ (**order**) supplies every Tuesday.

   She_____ (**look**) at the supply catalog right now.

6. Mr. Taylor usually _____ (**get**) to work at 7:30.

   It's 7:25, so right now he_____ (**park**) his car.

7. Sally and Edward _____ (**clean**) the supply room

   once a week. Right now they_____ (**sweep**) the floor.

8. I usually _____ (**drive**) the delivery van. At the

   moment I_____ (**pick up**) the mail at the post office.

Name_____

A. Read Misha's job application. Complete the sentences. Follow the example.

Education	
High School	Center Valley High
Graduated?	yes
Date of graduation	June 1999
Work History	
1. Current or last job	Midtown Pharmacy
Position	Cashier
Dates	June 1999 to present
2. Previous job	Silver Screen Cinema
Position	Usher
Dates	September 1996 to June 1999

1. Misha _____ finished _____ (finish) high school **one year ago/two years ago/etc.**

2. He _____ (start) working at the movie theater _____.

3. The pharmacy _____ (hire) Misha as a cashier _____.

4. He _____ (stop) working at the movie theater _____.

5. He _____ (quit) working at the pharmacy _____.

B. Complete the sentences. Write the correct form of the verb. Circle **for** or **since**.

1. We __'ve made__ (make) sugar-free cakes **for** /(**since**)1993.

2. I_____ (want) to transfer to the downtown store **for** / **since** the winter sales meeting.

3. You_____ (receive) three promotions **for** / **since** 1995.

4. Allen_____ (work) at the garage **for** / **since** last January.

5. We_____ (have) that toy in stock **for** / **since** two weeks.

6. They_____ (try) to fix the problem **for** / **since** 10:00.

7. She_____ (work) here **for** / **since** 1987.

8. I_____ (be) a truck driver **for** / **since** three years.

Blackline Masters

Name _____

A. Complete the sentences. Follow the example.

1. The sale fliers _____ **are mailed** _____ (mail) to customers two weeks before the sale.

2. The night before the sale, new price tags _____ (put) on the clothes.

3. On the day of the sale, the employees _____ (require) to come to work half an hour early.

4. When the sale is over, new merchandise _____ (send) to the store.

5. The night after the sale, the new merchandise _____ (put) on the shelves.

B. Complete the sentences. Follow the example.

1. Our vegetables are fresh. They _____ **were grown** _____ (grow) by a local farmer.

2. The delivery truck _____ (load) by Mark and Daniel.

3. The boxes _____ (open) by someone in the mail room.

4. All the employees _____ (hire) by the manager before the store opened.

5. The sign _____ (paint) by a professional painter.

6. The refreshments _____ (order) by our secretary.

7. The soup _____ (make) by the head cook.

8. The baggage _____ (bring) to your room by a bellhop.

C. Complete the sentences. Follow the examples.

1. I _____ **prefer to work** _____ (prefer/work) the day shift.

2. They _____ **prefer working** _____ (prefer/work) the night shift.

3. Jean _____ (like/help) new employees.

4. Don _____ (like/finish) his paperwork before he leaves.

5. Mai _____ (love/read) stories to the children.

6. They _____ (prefer/deliver) the orders themselves.

7. She _____ (not like/chop) onions.

8. They _____ (hate/drive) in the city.

Blackline Masters

Name _____

A. Write **by** or **without** and the correct form of the verb. Follow the example.

1. Turn off the VCR _____**by pressing**_____ (**press**) this switch.

2. I want to reuse the glass in the picture frame, so please remove the

   glass _____ (**break**) it.

3. Can you keep the soup hot _____ (**burn**) it?

4. You need to keep your workstation clean, so be careful to unpack the

   boxes _____ (**make**) a mess.

5. Janet is a good typist. She can type 65 words a minute
   _____ (**make**) any mistakes.

6. That nurse's aide is good with children. He makes them laugh

   _____ (**act**) silly. He can give them

   shots _____ (**make**) them cry.

7. Be careful to fry the eggs _____ (**break**) the yolks.

8. We can prevent workplace accidents _____ (**follow**) the
   safety rules.

B. Complete the sentences. Follow the example.

1. Don't leave _____**without**_____ (**by/without**) your tool belt.

2. We always check orders _____ (**by/without**) phone.

3. Dan fixed the door _____ (**without/by**) a screwdriver.

4. We serve every sandwich _____ (**with/by**) a pickle.

5. Steve sent the equipment _____ (**with/by**) train.

6. We locked the door _____ (**by/with**) mistake.

7. She painted all the signs herself, _____ (**by/without**) any help.

8. I commute to work _____ (**by/without**) car.

9. Patients are trying to sleep, so please complete the work

   _____ (**with/without**) making a lot of noise.

10. We won't accept returned merchandise _____ (**by/without**)
    a receipt.

A. Complete the dialog. Write **Who**, **What**, **When**, or **Where**.

1. **A** I heard that we're starting a new job soon. _____**What**'s the new job?

   B Fixing up an apartment building downtown.

2. **A** _____'s the job site?

   B On Western Avenue.

3. **A** _____'s on the crew?

   B The crew is Danny, Richard, Alfred, Ana, and Pablo.

4. **A** That's a good team. _____'s the team leader?

   B Marco. He has a lot of experience.

5. **A** _____ does the new job start?

   B March 26, I think.

6. **A** _____ will we finish?

   B I think we'll finish in about a month.

B. Rewrite the sentences. Use **who** or **that**. Follow the example.

1. I'm looking for the trash can. The trash can goes next to the dishwasher.

   I'm looking for the trash can that goes next to the dishwasher.

2. Jill just talked to a customer. The customer was happy with her work.

   _____

3. The manager has a checklist. The checklist lists all of today's work.

   _____

4. The package is with a driver. The driver delivers to that neighborhood.

   _____

5. We opened the boxes. The boxes came on this morning's truck.

   _____

6. We received the office supplies. The office supplies were ordered last week.

   _____

Name _____

A. Complete the sentences. Use **may** or **must**. Follow the example.

Early Learning **Day Care Center**		
	Required Activities	**Optional Activities**
Morning	Read a story to the children. Lead an organized activity, such as a game.	Have the children sing. Lead children on a nature walk. Invite a guest to talk to the children. Allow the children to play outside.
Lunch	Serve lunch by 11:45.	
Afternoon	Provide at least half an hour for naps or quiet time. Serve a nutritious snack.	Allow the children to play outside.

1. In the morning, the daycare worker _____*must*_____ read a story.

2. At Early Learning Day Care Center, teachers _____ serve lunch by 11:45.

3. The teacher _____ have the children sing.

4. The teacher _____ lead an organized activity in the morning.

5. The teacher _____ let the children play outside.

6. The children _____ have a snack during the day.

7. The children _____ take a nap or have quiet time every afternoon.

B. Complete the sentences. Circle **may** or **must**. Follow the example.

1. Employees **may** / **(must)** work for the company for six months before they can apply for a transfer.

2. We pay our workers by the hour. You **may** / **must** clock in and out to get paid.

3. How much flour the baker uses depends on the weather. She **may** / **must** need a little extra flour some days.

4. We don't have a dress code for food servers, so you **may** / **must** wear any clothes you want.

5. Welders **may** / **must** keep their work areas clear at all times. It's a safety rule.

6. You **may** / **must** close the safety latch to start the mixer. If you don't, the mixer won't start.

7. You **may** / **must** take your break now or at 10:15. It's your decision.

C. Complete the sentences. Follow the examples.

1. If you _____ *need* _____ (**need**) help unloading the truck in the

   morning, I _____ *could come* _____ (**come**) in early.

2. If the meeting _____ (**end**) before 5:00, the managers said

   we _____ (**leave**) early.

3. If we _____ (**not receive**) the parts by Friday,

   we _____ (**miss**) our deadline.

4. You _____ (**go**) to the store if

   we _____ (**run out**) of paper.

5. You have to wait for the blades to stop turning before you lift the handle.

   You _____ (**break**) the machine if you

   _____ (**not wait**).

6. If you _____ (**not remember**) the order,

   you _____ (**make**) a mistake.

7. If you _____ (**have**) a good one-year review,

   you _____ (**get**) a better raise.

8. The restaurant _____ (**fail**) the health inspection if

   we _____ (**not follow**) all the kitchen rules.

D. Complete the sentences. Follow the example.

1. _____ **Wearing** _____ (**Wear**) safety shoes is required in the factory.

2. _____ (**Climb**) on the shelves is not allowed.

3. _____ (**Talk**) to customers on the phone is part of your job.

4. _____ (**List**) the things I have to do everyday helps me stay organized.

5. _____ (**Drive**) is my favorite part of this job.

6. _____ (**Lift**) heavy boxes makes me tired.

7. _____ (**Write**) the schedule takes Lisa about an hour.

8. _____ (**Plant**) these trees is our first priority today.

A. Complete the sentences. Use the words in the box. Follow the example.

happy	tired	busy	worried	~~sad~~	sick

1. Raymond's company is closing. He _____ *must be sad* _____ .

2. Roberto has been on the phone all morning with customers.

   He _____ .

3. Lisa's son is sick today. She _____ .

4. Did you hear that Soo Lin just got a promotion? She _____ .

5. Antonio and Laura have unloaded boxes for six hours. They _____ .

6. Rhonda isn't in today. She _____ .

B. Give the people advice. Use **should**, **ought to**, or **had better**. Follow the example.

1. I think this sign has the wrong price on it.

   _____ **We should put the right price on it.** _____

2. She doesn't eat lunch. But she gets really tired in the afternoon.

   _____

3. I thought I did everything, but the customer said I didn't paint all the trim.

   _____

4. Her children don't have school next week. She'd like to take some time off to be

   with them. _____

5. He forgot to bring the VCR to the conference room.

   _____

6. We don't have enough hard hats for all the workers on the first shift.

   _____

7. The air compressor won't start.

   _____

© Steck-Vaughn Company. *English ASAP Level 4.* Permission granted to reproduce for classroom use.

Blackline Masters

Name _____

A. Complete the sentences. Follow the example.

1. _____ *Taking* _____ (**Take**) night classes allows me to go to school while I'm working full-time.

2. It's nice _____ *to smile* _____ (**smile**) when you answer the phone.

3. _____ (**Break**) a large job into small tasks helps get the job done.

4. It's a good idea _____ (**organize**) your work area.

5. It's important _____ (**find out**) what your customers want.

6. _____ (**Interview**) for a job makes me nervous.

7. It's your responsibility _____ (**talk**) to your supervisor if you have a problem with the schedule.

8. It's important _____ (**complete**) the work order for every job.

9. _____ (**Add**) breakfast sandwiches to our menu was a good idea.

10. _____ (**Help**) other workers is a good way to find out what kind of job you want to have.

11. It's dangerous _____ (**stand**) near the punch presses.

B. Rewrite the sentences.

1. It's easy to make bread.

   Making bread is easy. _____

2. Planning your schedule is important.

   _____

3. Changing the oil in a car takes about 20 minutes.

   _____

4. It's exciting to get a promotion.

   _____

5. It's dangerous to enter the worksite without a hard hat.

   _____

C. Complete Miguel's resume.

Resume
Miguel Benitez

EXPERIENCE

Present

Prep Cook, Antonio's Restaurant, 1999–Present

- _____**Preparing**_____ (**Prepare**) salads.

- _____ (**Cut**) and _____ (**slice**) vegetables.

- _____ (**Clean**) pots and pans.

- _____ (**Make**) soup and side dishes.

- _____ (**Wash**) counters and cutting boards.

Past Jobs

Bus Person, The Uptown Cafe, 1997–1999

- _____**Cleared**_____ (**Clear**) dishes from tables.

- _____ (**Bring**) dirty dishes to the kitchen.

- _____ (**Take**) clean silverware to the dining room.

- _____ (**Serve**) chips, salsa, and water to customers.

- _____ (**Clean**) the dining room at the end of the shift.

Dishwasher, The Uptown Cafe, 1995–1997

- _____ (**Wash**) cups, glasses, plates, and silverware.

- _____ (**Put away**) clean dishes.

- _____ (**Fix**) the automatic dishwasher.

A. Write about what the people do at their jobs. Use the correct form of the verb.

1. They _____washed_____ (**wash**) the car a few minutes ago.

   Now they __'re waxing__ (**wax**) the car.

   Next they __'re going to vacuum__ (**vacuum**) the interior.

2. Linda just _____ (**wash**) the customer's hair.

   Now Mauricio_____ (**cut**) the customer's hair.

   Next he_____ (**dry**) the customer's hair.

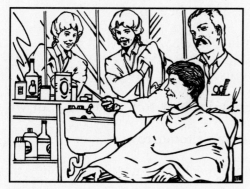

3. They _____ (**start**) cleaning the pool half an hour ago.

   Right now Rodney_____ (**remove**) leaves from the water.

   Ravi_____ (**scrub**) the walkways after they finish cleaning the pool.

4. They_____ (**set**) the tables right now.

   Susie _____ (**fold**) the napkins earlier. Now she

   _____ (**place**) them on the table.

   Maria_____ (**fill**) the water glasses right before the guests arrive.

B. Complete the sentences. Follow the example.

1. If I _____ **have** _____ (have) time, I _'ll check_ _____ (check) all

   the lights to make sure the bulbs aren't burned out. This morning I

   _____ (notice) that one of the lights on the balcony is out.

   I _____ (change) the bulb later today.

2. John _____ (place) an order later this afternoon. If you

   _____ (need) any supplies, he _____ (order)

   them. He _____ (get) more paint, because I

   _____ (use) all the paint last week when I

   _____ (make) the sale signs.

3. Jamie and Mike _____ (explain) how to use the new air wrench

   later today. Steve _____ (use) it tomorrow.

4. They _____ (hire) two more mechanics next week. They think

   the garage _____ (be) really busy during the summer. Last

   summer they _____ (not have) enough people. So last summer

   everyone _____ (work) a lot of overtime.

5. I _____ (be) a bus driver for five years. I _____

   (like) driving a bus. Right now I _____ (drive) on Green Street.

   I _____ (pick up) some regular passengers in a few minutes.

   They _____ (take) the bus every day.

6. April 15 _____ (be) last week, so we all

   _____ (file) our tax returns. In a few weeks,

   I _____ (get) a refund check.

7. Last week Jennie _____ (order) the notebooks we need.

   Yesterday Melissa _____ (type) the manuscript. If the notebooks

   _____ (arrive) today, Jeanne _____ (photocopy) the

   manuscript and put it in the notebooks.

Blackline Masters — Answer Key

UNIT 1

A.
1. used to cook
2. cooks
3. drives
4. used to drive
5. used to sell
6. sells
7. cleans
8. used to clean

B.
1. was washing, started
2. arrived, was cleaning
3. was counting, turned off
4. fell, was unloading
5. rang, was sleeping

C.
1. stayed
2. took
3. didn't finish
4. took
5. told
6. sewed
7. finished, started
8. didn't fix, bought, didn't install
9. got
10. didn't write, wrote

D.
took out
swept
went
paid
found
made
mopped
fixed

UNIT 2

A.
1. feels upset
2. feel hungry
3. feels happy
4. feel disappointed
5. feels tired

B.
1. takes, 's waiting
2. makes, 's cooking
3. works, 's ringing up
4. helps, 's preparing
5. orders, 's looking
6. gets, 's parking
7. clean, 're sweeping
8. drive, 'm picking up

UNIT 3

A.
1. finished, one year ago/two years ago/etc.
2. started, *answers will vary*
3. hired, *answers will vary*

4. stopped, *answers will vary*
5. quit, *answers will vary*

B.
1. 've made, since
2. 've wanted, since
3. 've received, since
4. 's worked, since
5. 've had, for
6. 've tried, since
7. 's worked, since
8. 've been, for

UNIT 4

A.
1. are mailed
2. are put
3. are required
4. is sent
5. is put

B.
1. were grown
2. was loaded
3. were opened
4. were hired
5. was painted
6. were ordered
7. was made
8. was brought

C.
1. prefer to work *or* prefer working
2. prefer to work *or* prefer working
3. likes to help *or* likes helping
4. likes to finish *or* likes finishing
5. loves to read *or* loves reading
6. prefer to deliver *or* prefer delivering
7. doesn't like to chop *or* doesn't like chopping
8. hate to drive *or* hate driving

UNIT 5

A.
1. by pressing
2. without breaking
3. without burning
4. without making
5. without making
6. by acting, without making
7. without breaking
8. by following

B.
1. without
2. by
3. without
4. with
5. by
6. by
7. without
8. by
9. without
10. without

English ASAP

UNIT 6

A.
1. What
2. Where
3. Who
4. Who
5. When
6. When

B.
1. I'm looking for the trash can that goes next to the dishwasher.
2. Jill just talked to a customer who was happy with her work.
3. The manager has a checklist that lists all of today's work.
4. The package is with a driver who delivers to that neighborhood.
5. We opened the boxes that came on this morning's truck.
6. We received the office supplies that were ordered last week.

UNIT 7

A.
1. must
2. must
3. may
4. must
5. may
6. must
7. must

B.
1. must
2. must
3. may
4. may
5. must
6. must
7. may

C.
1. need, could come
2. ends, could leave
3. don't receive, could miss
4. could go, run out
5. could break, don't wait
6. don't remember, could make
7. have, could get
8. could fail, don't follow

D.
1. Wearing
2. Climbing
3. Talking
4. Listing
5. Driving
6. Lifting
7. Writing
8. Planting

UNIT 8

A.
1. must be sad
2. must be busy
3. must be worried
4. must be happy
5. must be tired
6. must be sick

B. *Many answers are possible but may include the following:*
1. We should put the right price on it.
2. She should eat lunch.
3. You ought to check your work more carefully.
4. She'd better ask for time off right away.
5. He'd better get the VCR.
6. We'd better order more hard hats.
7. We ought to call a repair person.

UNIT 9

A.
1. Taking
2. to smile
3. Breaking
4. to organize
5. to find out
6. Interviewing
7. to talk
8. to complete
9. Adding
10. Helping
11. to stand

B.
1. Making bread is easy.
2. It's important to plan your schedule.
3. It takes about 20 minutes to change the oil in a car.
4. Getting a promotion is exciting.
5. Entering the worksite without a hard hat is dangerous.

C.
Preparing
Cutting, slicing
Cleaning
Making
Washing
Cleared
Brought
Took
Served
Cleaned
Washed
Put away
Fixed

UNIT 10

A.
1. washed, 're waxing, 're going to vacuum
2. washed, 's cutting, 's going to dry
3. started, 's removing, 's going to scrub
4. 're setting, folded, 's placing, 's going to fill

B.
1. have, 'll check, noticed, 'm going to change
2. 's going to place, need, 'll order, 's going to get, used, made
3. are going to explain, 's going to use
4. 're going to hire, 's going to be, didn't have, worked
5. 've been, like, 'm driving, 'm going to pick up, take
6. was, filed, 'm going to get
7. ordered, typed, arrive, 's going to photocopy

English ASAP

Learner _____

Class _____

Teacher _____

Individual Competency Chart

Unit 1

	Date Presented	Date Checked	Result (✔)	Comments
1. Summarize information				
2. Put information in order				
3. Ask for information				
4. Interpret information				

Unit 2

	Date Presented	Date Checked	Result (✔)	Comments
1. Describe your job duties				
2. Explain why your job is important				
3. Transfer your skills to a better job				
4. Learn from experience				

Unit 3

	Date Presented	Date Checked	Result (✔)	Comments
1. Put information in a computer				
2. Get information from a computer				
3. Understand information from a computer				
4. Use information from a computer				

Individual Competency Chart

Unit 4

	Date Presented	Date Checked	Result (✔)	Comments
1. Set short-term and long-term goals				
2. Deal with setbacks				
3. Set priorities				
4. Avoid procrastination				

Unit 5

	Date Presented	Date Checked	Result (✔)	Comments
1. Respond positively to customers' complaints				
2. Solve customers' problems				
3. Evaluate advice about customer service				
4. Improve customer service				

Unit 6

	Date Presented	Date Checked	Result (✔)	Comments
1. Understand how your workplace is organized				
2. Identify bosses, coworkers, and direct reports				
3. Identify training needs				
4. Develop a plan for solving a problem				

Individual Competency Chart

Individual Competency Chart

Learner _____

Class _____

Teacher _____

Unit 7

		Date Presented	Date Checked	Result (✔)	Comments
1.	Interpret and evaluate a budget				
2.	Create a budget				
3.	Adjust a budget				
4.	Make decisions on a budget				

Unit 8

		Date Presented	Date Checked	Result (✔)	Comments
1.	Identify health and safety problems				
2.	Solve health and safety problems				
3.	Improve health and safety				

Individual Competency Chart

Learner _____

Class _____

Teacher _____

Unit 9

	Date Presented	Date Checked	Result (✔)	Comments
1. Confirm information before you act				
2. Demonstrate leadership skills				
3. Adjust to change				

Unit 10

	Date Presented	Date Checked	Result (✔)	Comments
1. Evaluate job performance				
2. Assess your work skills				
3. Plan for the future				

Individual Competency Chart